Candle
BIBLE
for Kids

Juliet David
Illustrated by Jo Parry

CANDLE
BOOKS

Contents

New Testament

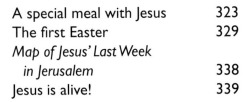

Old Testament

God creates the world

In the beginning God made heaven and earth. He made it all.

At first there were no people. No animals. No light. Nothing…
It was dark and empty.

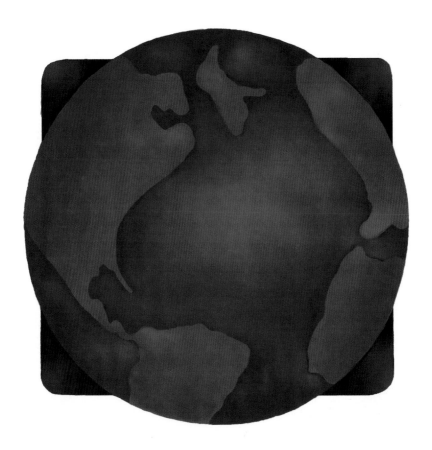

Then God said, "Let there be light!" And there was light.

God separated the light from darkness and called it "day". The darkness he called "night".

So there was day and night.

God did all this on day one.

The next day God poured water into the sea. He blew air and clouds into the sky.

Now there was water and air.

God did all this on day two.

On day three God was very busy. He gathered up the water so that land appeared. He made oceans and lakes, waterfalls and rivers. He made dry land – hills and plains and valleys.

Then God said, "Let the earth be green." And grass and flowers and tall trees sprang up. So many kinds that no one could count them.

And God said, "It is all good."

On day four God said: "Let there be lights in the sky! They will divide time into days and months and years."

So he put the sun in the sky.

God saw that night was very dark, so he put the moon and stars in the sky. That night they came out for the very first time.

God said, "It is all good."

On day five, God filled the sea with fish. He made starfish, eels, whales, and turtles. Fast little fish for the rivers and big floppy fish for the oceans. And God filled the sky with birds. Great eagles, skimming hummingbirds, and squawking parrots. He made birds of all shapes, sizes, and hues.

And God said, "It is all good."

On day six God said, "Now let there be life on the earth!"
So he made the animals – cows, horses, turtles, and bears,
lizards, mice, worms, and lots more. But there were no people.

So God made the first man, Adam. And the first woman,
Eve. He made them to be his friends. "Look after the fish, the
birds, and all the other creatures," he told them.

God saw everything he had created. It was all just right.

Then on day seven God rested. No more creating!
And that's how God created the heavens and the earth.

Genesis 1–2

Adam and Eve leave the garden

God put Adam and Eve in a beautiful garden called Eden. "Give names to the animals I have created," God told them. What fun they had making up names! Alligators and caterpillars, elephants and tortoises, squirrels and porpoises.

"Enjoy yourselves," God told Adam and Eve. "Eat anything you like in the garden."

But he warned them: "Never ever eat fruit from that *special* tree in the middle of the garden."

So Adam and Eve started to explore. They ate fruit. They sat beside streams. They walked through the trees. They lay in the soft grass. And they looked after the creatures living in the garden.

One day a sneaky snake slithered up to Eve. "Sssssss," he sneered. "Why don't you eat the fruit on *that* tree?"

"But that's the fruit God told us never to eat," said Eve.

"Ssssssss," hissed the snake again. "Just take a bite."

"No – I really shouldn't," said Eve.

"Just one teeny, tiny bite. It won't matter."

So Eve did take a bite of the fruit from the forbidden tree.
Then Adam came to find Eve.

"Here, taste this fruit," said Eve. "I have — and it didn't hurt me at all."

She gave the fruit to Adam. He bit into the forbidden fruit too.

That afternoon God came to the garden. Adam and Eve were hiding. "Where are you?" God called. He soon found them.

"Why are you hiding?" he asked.

"Eve gave me the fruit – so I ate it," said Adam.

"The snake tricked me," explained Eve, trying to blame someone else too. "That's why I ate the fruit."

God was sad. Adam and Eve had disobeyed him. So God sent them both out of the beautiful garden. For ever.

He ordered angels with flashing swords to stop Adam and Eve sneaking back into Eden.

Never again would they see the beautiful flowers or enjoy quiet walks beside the peaceful rivers.

Adam and Eve felt very sorry and very sad.

Now Adam and Eve had to work hard. They had to grow food. They sowed seeds, tore up weeds, and tended plants. The ground was rough. Thistles grew everywhere.

Day after day they worked. Digging and sowing, hoeing and raking, weeding and watering. It was hard, tiring work.

How different from the Garden of Eden!

Genesis 3

Noah and the rainbow

Adam and Eve had children, and their children married and had children too. Years passed and many people lived on the earth.

Adam and Eve, their children, and their children's children knew good from evil. Some chose good. Some chose evil, and argued and hurt each other. It became a bad world. God became sorry he had made it.

But there was one good man on the earth: Noah.

"I'm going to destroy the earth," God told Noah. "I will flood the whole world with water."

"Can I escape?" asked Noah.

"Yes – I will save you and your family and the animals," said God. "But first you must build a great wooden ship – an ark." And then God explained just how to make the ark.

So Noah and his sons – Shem, Ham, and Japheth – started to build. They cut down trees. They sawed branches. They hammered planks. They worked as hard as they could, because the ark had to be the biggest ship ever.

"Why are you building a ship on dry land?" Noah's friends asked. "Have you gone mad?!"

"Soon floods will come," Noah explained. "Water will cover the earth – but we'll be safe in our ark."

"You're crazy!" they said, and laughed rudely.

But Noah and his sons went on sawing and hammering.

"You must take two of every creature into the ark," God told Noah. So Noah and his sons collected two lions, two giraffes, two elephants, two mice, two flamingoes, two tiny spiders – two of everything.

Suddenly the weather changed. "It's time to enter the ark," said Noah. In went Noah, his family, and all the creatures, two by two. God shut the door. Then the floods came.

The rain fell and didn't stop. The water rose higher and higher. Soon the ark was afloat – with Noah, his family, and all the animals safe inside. They sailed in the ark for forty days. Then at last the rain stopped. Slowly, the water began to go down.

Bump! Crash! "We've landed on a mountain," said Noah. "I'll send out a raven." The raven flew off. It never came back. It just kept flying until the water dried up.

Next Noah sent out a dove. By evening she was back – there was nowhere for her to perch.

A week later Noah sent off the dove again. This time she returned with a green branch in her beak. Noah knew the water had gone down.

Noah sent out the dove a third time. She didn't come back. The floods had all gone.

"Now you can leave the ark," God told Noah. So Noah, his family, and all the creatures left the ark. The animals scampered away.

God said, "Never again will I flood the earth. There will always be sowing and harvest, summer, and winter. I will put a special sign in the sky to remind you." So God put a rainbow in the sky. When we see it, we remember how God saved Noah from the flood.

Genesis 6–9

Abraham makes a new start

Long ago, in a far-off land called Ur, there lived a man named Abram. He was married to Sarah. Abram and Sarah were already old, but they had no children.

One day Abram heard God speaking to him.

"Leave your home!" God told him. "You must take a long journey. I'm going to give you a special new land."

Abram and Sarah were brave. They believed God and were ready to leave home. They set out, taking with them their servants, their camels, their cattle, and their sheep.

Abram had no map for the journey. God told him, "I will show you how to get to the land I promised you. I will make you the father of a great people."

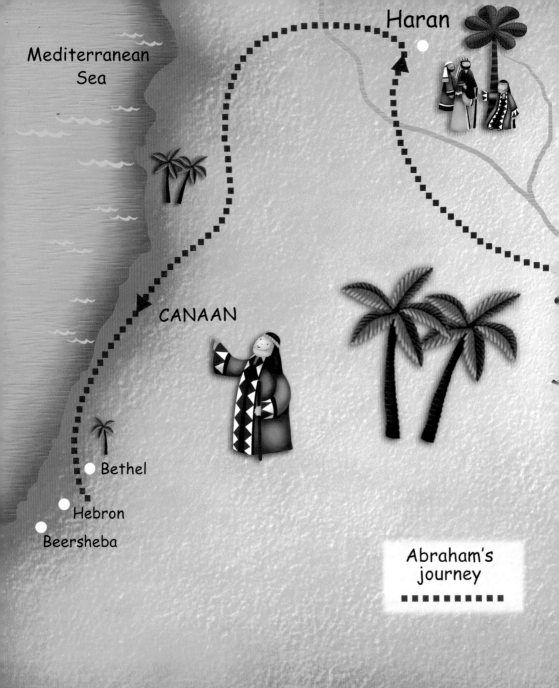

Mediterranean
Sea

Haran

CANAAN

Bethel

Hebron

Beersheba

Abraham's
journey

Abraham's Travels

MESOPOTAMIA

River Euphrates

River Tigris

Babylon

BABYLONIA

Ur

After journeying for many months, Abram came at last to the land that God had promised. It was called "Canaan". In Canaan there were lush, green valleys and fast-flowing rivers.

"This is the country I told you about!" God said to Abram. "I'm giving this land to you, to your children, and your grandchildren."

Abram had brought with him his nephew, Lot. But Lot kept arguing with Abram. Lot wanted to have all the best land for his own sheep and goats.

Tired of all the quarrels, Abram said generously, "All right, Lot – you take the best land."

Now Abram and Sarah settled down to live in their new land. Abram's flocks of sheep grew huge and his herds of camels even larger. Soon he became very rich. But Abram always remembered God's promise: *One day you will have many children, grandchildren, and great-grandchildren.*

By now Sarah was too old to have children.

Abram complained to God, "We've been waiting so long for a family."

Then one night God told Abram to go outside. "Look at the stars in the sky!" he said.

Abram looked up.

"Can you count the stars?" God asked.

Abram shook his head.

"You will have as many children, grandchildren, and great-grandchildren as there are stars in the night sky," said God.

And Abram believed God.

It was Abram's ninety-ninth birthday. To celebrate, God changed Abram's name to "Abraham".

Not long after, Abraham was sitting in his tent. It was midday and the sun was burning hot. Three men Abraham had never seen before appeared.

"Come and sit in the shade," Abraham called out. "It's cooler here. Please eat with me."

"Quick! Bake some bread!" Abraham told Sarah. "Cook a feast!"

When lunch was ready, they sat down to eat and drink. One of the visitors asked Abraham, "Where's Sarah?"

"She's inside the tent," Abraham answered.

"Next year Sarah will have a baby," the visitor told him. "A baby boy."

Sarah was listening through the wall of the tent. She just laughed. She heard what the stranger said – but she didn't believe a word of it.

I can't possibly have children at my age, Sarah told herself.

"Why did Sarah laugh?" the stranger asked Abraham. "Nothing is impossible for God."

Sure enough, about a year later Sarah had a baby boy – just as God promised.

Sarah was so happy. "God has made me laugh," she said. "Everyone who hears this will want to laugh too."

So Sarah named her baby Isaac – which means "laughter".

Genesis 12–18, 21

A wife for Isaac

Isaac grew up to be a fine young man. He helped his father, Abraham, look after his flocks of sheep and herds of cattle.

The day came when Abraham thought Isaac should find a wife.

So Abraham called for his trusted servant, Eliezer.

"Go back to the land we came from," Abraham told him. "When you are there find a good wife for my son, Isaac."

So Abraham's servant loaded his camels with rich gifts and set out on the long, dusty journey to find a wife for Isaac.

At last Eliezer arrived in the land Abraham had come from.

He suddenly thought, *I've no idea how I'm going to find a wife for Isaac!* He sat beside a well to ponder his problem.

Then God said to Eliezer, "The woman who gives your camels water to drink will be Isaac's wife."

Not long after a beautiful young woman came to the well, carrying a water pot.

"Sir, would you like water for your camels?" she asked politely. At once Eliezer knew this must be the woman God had chosen as Isaac's wife.

"What is your name?" he asked.

"I'm called Rebekah," she said. "Come home and meet my family."

When he arrived, Eliezer took out the gifts he had brought and gave them to Rebekah's family. Then he asked her father. "Will you let your beautiful daughter Rebekah marry Abraham's son?"

"With pleasure!" he answered.

So Rebekah packed her belongings and set off for Canaan with Eliezer.

The journey took many days. Then one evening, just before sunset, they stopped. A young man was walking in the fields. He looked up. It was Isaac! He saw the beautiful young woman riding one of the camels. His bride had come! Isaac loved Rebekah very much – and married her.

Genesis 24

The troublesome twins

Isaac and Rebekah were soon happily married. But they had no children. So Isaac and Rebekah prayed to God.

It wasn't long before Rebekah was expecting twins. The firstborn twin was red and very hairy. They named him Esau. But Jacob, the second twin, had soft, smooth skin.

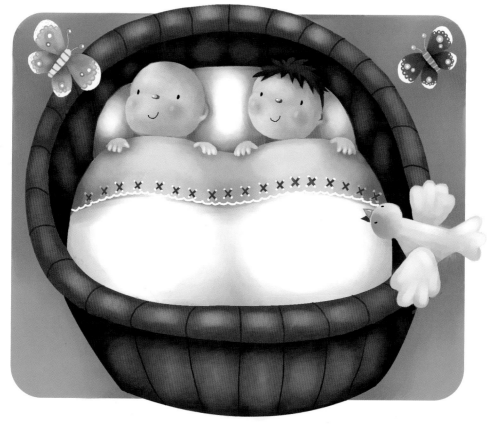

Esau grew up bold and fearless. He loved to go out hunting. But Jacob preferred to stay at home with Rebekah. He was full of tricks.

One day Esau came home very hungry. He saw Jacob cooking stew. "Give me some of that!" said Esau. "I'm starving!"

Thinking quickly, Jacob said, "Give me your rights as Isaac's oldest son – and you can have my stew."

"All right," said Esau foolishly.

Isaac grew old and blind. He wanted to give his special blessing to his older son, Esau. But Rebekah wanted Jacob to get this blessing, so she tied hairy animal skin to Jacob's arms.

"Father, give me your special blessing," said Jacob, when Esau was away.

"Stretch out your arms," said Isaac. "If they're hairy, I'll know you're Esau." Jacob held out his arms – they felt hairy. Isaac thought it was Esau and gave Jacob his special blessing.

When Esau came in, he was furious.

"Jacob has stolen my blessing!" he cried. "Where is he?"

But Jacob had gone! He'd run away to his uncle, who lived in a far-off country.

One night while he was on the run, Jacob slept in the desert, using a rock for a pillow. He had a wonderful dream. Jacob saw a stairway to heaven, with angels walking up and down. God promised him, "I will always look after your family."

When Jacob woke up, he said, "God is in this place!"

At last, Jacob reached his uncle Laban's house. Laban had two daughters, Leah and Rachel. Before long, Jacob fell in love with Rachel. He wanted to marry her.

"Work for me for seven years," said Laban, "then you may marry my daughter."

Jacob worked hard every day so that he could marry the woman he loved. At last the wedding day arrived. The bride wore a veil hiding her face.

But after they were married, she took off the veil. Jacob had a shock. It was Leah – not Rachel! Laban had tricked him. He'd given Jacob his older daughter as his wife – not Rachel.

Jacob was very angry. But Laban said, "Work seven years more – then I'll give you Rachel."

Jacob loved Rachel so much he worked for Laban seven more years. Then at last he married his beloved.

Now Jacob decided it was time to go home. When he was almost there, Esau came to meet him. Was he still angry with Jacob? Esau ran up to him and hugged him. After this, the quarrelsome brothers lived as friends.

Genesis 25, 27–29, 33

Joseph and his brothers

Jacob had a big family of twelve sons. He loved every one of them. But Jacob loved his young son Joseph more than all the others.

One day Jacob gave Joseph a fantastic coat. How smart he looked! His brothers felt very jealous. Why should Joseph get all the best presents?

Sometimes Joseph had strange dreams. He loved to describe them to his brothers.

"I had the weirdest dream," he told them one day. "We each had a bundle of grain. Then your bundles of grain all bowed down to mine."

Joseph's brothers were cross. "So you think we should all bow down to you?" asked one.

"You're no better than us," said another.

Some time later Jacob called for Joseph.

"Your brothers have gone away with the sheep," he said. "Take some food to them." So off Joseph went.

Joseph's brothers saw him coming.

"Here comes our brother, the dreamer!" said one.

"Let's get rid of him," said another.

But a kinder brother said, "Don't hurt Joseph. Let's throw him down this dry well." He planned to rescue Joseph when his brothers had gone.

When Joseph arrived, his brothers ripped off his coat and threw him into the well. Then they saw some traders passing. "Let's sell Joseph!" said one brother.

So they sold their young brother Joseph. They took his torn coat to old Jacob.

"Look, father," they said, pretending to be sad. "We found Joseph's special coat – the one you gave him. A wild animal must have killed him."

No one could comfort Jacob.

Meanwhile the traders took Joseph to the land of Egypt.
Joseph was sad. Never again would he see the people he loved.
The traders brought Joseph to a market where people came
to buy slaves. A rich Egyptian called Potiphar saw Joseph and
bought him to work in his house.

Joseph worked hard for Potiphar. But Potiphar's wife came to dislike Joseph, so she lied about him to her husband.

Potiphar threw Joseph into prison.

But in prison, everyone liked Joseph. Before long, the governor put Joseph in charge of his prison.

The king's cup-bearer and the king's baker were thrown into prison. One night, both men had strange dreams. What did they mean? They asked Joseph.

Joseph explained to the cup-bearer, "In three days Pharaoh, king of Egypt, will send for you and you will work for him again." Then Joseph spoke to the baker. "I'm sorry, but your dream means that Pharaoh will have you put to death."

"Please remember me when you see Pharaoh," said Joseph to the cup-bearer as he left prison. "I don't want to stay in prison the rest of my life."

But the cup-bearer forgot all about Joseph once he was back in Pharaoh's palace.

Then one night Pharaoh had two strange dreams. He described his dreams to his wise men.

"I saw seven fat cows come out of the river," said Pharaoh. "Then seven skinny cows swallowed up the seven fat cows. In my second dream seven good ears of grain were growing. Then seven bad ears ate up the good ears of grain. Whatever do my dreams mean?"

"We don't know," said the wise men – so Pharaoh sent them all away.

At that very moment the cup-bearer remembered Joseph.

"O, Pharaoh!" he said, "in your prison is a young man who can explain dreams."

"Then send for him at once!"

Soon Joseph was standing before Pharaoh dressed in new clothes.

"I will tell you my dreams," said Pharaoh. "Then you must explain to me what they mean."

So Pharaoh told his dreams again.

Joseph said, "Both dreams mean the same thing. The seven fat cows are seven years of rich harvests; the seven skinny cows are seven years with no harvest. The seven good ears of grain are also seven years of plenty, and the seven poor ears are seven hungry years."

"God sent these dreams to warn you," Joseph told Pharaoh. "In the seven years of plenty, everyone will have enough to eat. But in the seven years of hunger, there will be no food."

Pharaoh looked worried.

"You've explained my dreams," he said. "Now tell me how to stop my people starving in the bad years."

"Find a wise man to rule Egypt for you," said Joseph. "He must build storehouses and hoard part of the harvest in the good years until the bad years come. Then open up the storehouses and sell the grain to the hungry, so they can make bread to eat."

Pharaoh chose Joseph to become his chief minister! He took off his royal ring and put it on Joseph's finger.

For the next seven years, Joseph stored part of the harvest in great barns. When the hungry years came, the barns were opened and the people were given grain. The Egyptians had enough food even during the worst of the famine.

When the hungry years came, Jacob and his family in Canaan had no grain. But Jacob heard there was food in Egypt.

"Go to Egypt and buy grain," he told his sons. Benjamin, his youngest, stayed at home with old Jacob.

When Joseph saw his brothers, he knew who they were – but they didn't recognize him.

"You're spies!" he said, to test them.

"No!" they replied. "We've simply come to buy food."

Joseph gave them food, but said if they returned, they must bring Benjamin.

The brothers took the grain back to Jacob. But soon they needed more. The brothers returned to Egypt, taking Benjamin with them.

Joseph hid a silver cup in Benjamin's sack of grain, then cried, "My silver cup's missing! Who stole it?"

When they found the cup in Benjamin's sack, Joseph said Benjamin couldn't go home with the others. But his brothers begged Joseph not to keep Benjamin in Egypt. "It will kill our father, Jacob," they wept.

Joseph saw that his brothers had changed. They were no longer cruel, as they had been when they sold him years before.

"I'm Joseph, your brother," he told them. "You once sold me. Now hurry home and bring father to Egypt."

How glad Jacob was to find his beloved son Joseph again!

This is how God's people, the Israelites, came to live in Egypt.

Genesis 37, 39–47

The baby in the basket

After Jacob's family had been living in Egypt for many years, there came a new king, who hated the Israelites. This king, another Pharaoh, said, "There are too many of these Israelites. They're too strong. We'll make them work hard for us."

So Pharaoh forced the Israelites to make bricks and build him great cities. His soldiers beat the Israelites to make them work harder.

Then Pharaoh gave a terrible order: "Take every Israelite baby boy and throw him into the river," he said. "No more Israelite men will grow up in Egypt."

An Israelite mother called Jochebed had a baby boy. She was afraid that Egyptian soldiers would snatch him away. At first she hid the baby in her house. But she feared a passing Egyptian soldier might hear him crying.

So Jochebed made a plan. "We'll make a basket from rushes," she explained to her daughter, Miriam. "Then we'll float it in the river."

So Miriam and her mother made a strong basket. When it was finished, they put the baby in and hurried down to the river.

"Let's put him among the reeds," said Miriam.

"Now hide nearby and watch what happens," Jochebed told Miriam.

After a time, Miriam heard voices. She peeped out and saw the princess coming to bathe. Suddenly, the princess glimpsed something in the reeds.

"What's that?" she asked. "Please fetch it for me." Her maid ran to lift out the basket and took it to her mistress.

"What a beautiful baby!" she said. "It must be an Israelite boy who was to be thrown into the river. I wish he were mine."

Miriam crept up and stood beside the princess.

"Would you like a nurse for the baby?" she asked shyly.
"I know someone who could look after him."

The princess looked at the baby and decided to keep him.

"Go!" she said to Miriam. "Bring me a nurse for the boy."

Miriam ran home. "The princess found our baby," said Miriam happily. "She wants a nurse to look after him – come back with me."

Jochebed hurried to the river. "Are you looking for a nurse for the child?" she asked.

"Yes," smiled the princess, "I am. When he's old enough, I will make him my own son. Can you look after him until he grows into a boy?"

Jochebed was so happy!

"Look after him well," the princess told her. "When the time comes, bring him to live with me."

Jochebed and Miriam went off happily. Now their baby would grow up safely at home with them.

One day Jochebed took her son to the princess. The princess was proud of the boy. "I shall call you 'Moses'," she said. "That means 'taken from the water'."

Now Moses was brought up as a prince in the palace. He wore fine clothes and ate splendid food. But Moses never forgot that he was the son of an Israelite. He felt sorry for his people when he saw them working hard in the hot sun.

"When the time is right," he thought, "I will rescue them."

Exodus 1–2

Moses and Pharaoh

One day Moses saw an Egyptian beating an Israelite workman.
Moses was so angry that he killed the Egyptian. Then he fled
Egypt and lived as a shepherd in the desert.

Back in Egypt, Pharaoh made life even harder for the Israelites.
How they longed to escape.

As Moses was leading his flock of sheep, he saw a bush on fire. Although the bush was burning, it didn't burn away.

Then a voice called, "Moses! Moses! I am the God of Abraham." Moses trembled.

"The Egyptians are oppressing my people, the Israelites," said God. "I want you – Moses – to go to Pharaoh and tell him to let my people go."

"I couldn't do that!" said Moses.

"I will help you."

"But I stammer and stutter. Please send someone else!" pleaded Moses.

"Take your brother Aaron with you – he's a great speaker," said God. So Moses left his sheep and returned to Egypt.

Moses and Aaron stood before Pharaoh, king of Egypt.

"O Pharaoh," said Aaron. "God says: 'Let my people go so that they can worship me in the desert.'"

"I don't know this God of yours," shouted Pharaoh. "And I'm certainly not letting the Israelites go free!"

Then he ordered, "Make these Israelites work even harder."

"Pharaoh is making my people work harder still," Moses complained to God.

"Then go back and warn him," God told Moses. "If he doesn't let my people go, the Egyptians will suffer."

So Moses and Aaron returned to Pharaoh. Aaron threw down his stick and it turned into a snake. Pharaoh's magicians threw down their sticks too – and they also turned into snakes. But Aaron's snake gobbled up the rest of the snakes.

Still Pharaoh didn't do what God said.

So God sent very hard times on Egypt.

Moses and Aaron went to Pharaoh again. "God says: 'Let my people go,'" said Aaron. "If you don't, he'll turn the river to blood."

"I will not let your people go," replied Pharaoh.

So God turned the water of the River Nile to blood. No one could drink it.

"Ask your God to turn the blood back to water," said Pharaoh, "*then* I will let your people go."

God did so. But still Pharaoh didn't let the Israelites go.

After this God sent hordes of frogs all over the land.
Still Pharaoh did not let the people go.
God sent swarms of flies across the land.
Still Pharaoh did not let the Israelites go.
God made all the animals in Egypt fall sick.
Still Pharaoh did not let God's people go.

Painful sores appeared on the Egyptians' skin.

Huge hailstones fell on their fields. Grasshoppers called locusts ate every leaf and every stalk of grain.

Darkness fell across the entire land of Egypt.

Still Pharaoh did not obey God.

Finally God told Moses, "The firstborn of everything living in Egypt will die. To escape this, the Israelites must mark their doorways with lamb's blood."

So the Israelites splashed their doorways with lamb's blood.

At last Pharaoh told Moses, "Get your people out of Egypt."

So the Israelites left. Moses led his people out of Egypt on the long journey to the land that God had promised them.

In later years, the Israelites remembered that God saved them, in a festival they called "Passover".

Exodus 3–12

Out of Egypt

The Israelites walked day and night to get away from Egypt. But when they had gone, the Egyptians were furious. Now they had no one to work for them. So Pharaoh's army chased the Israelites.

The Israelites reached the shores of the Red Sea. But how were they to get across? The Egyptians were close behind…

"Don't be afraid!" said Moses. "God will help us."

He stretched out his hand and the waters divided. The Israelites walked safely across on dry land.

Then Moses lowered his hand, the water flowed back, and Pharaoh and his soldiers were drowned. At last the Israelites were safe from Pharaoh and the Egyptians.

But before long the Israelites ran out of food. They came angrily to Moses.

"Why did you lead us into the desert?" they shouted. "We'll starve to death here! We should have stayed in Egypt!"

"God will take care of you," said Moses. "Wait until morning – then you'll see something wonderful!"

When they woke, the Israelites saw white powder covering the ground. It tasted good! They called it "manna" and found it every morning.

The Israelites trudged for weeks through the desert. Tired and hot, they came to Mount Sinai, where they set up camp. Moses climbed the mountain to meet with God.

"I will be your God and you shall be my people," he promised. "I will give you rules for living. Write them down."

So Moses wrote down God's rules on flat stones. We call them the "Ten Commandments".

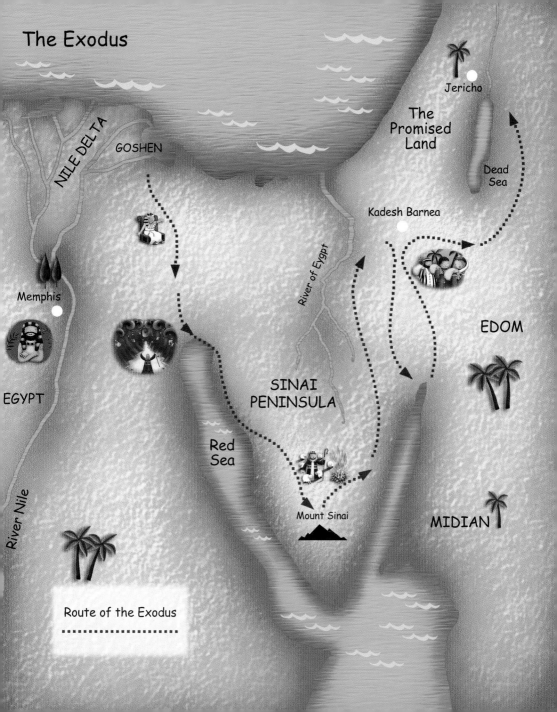

Moses was away on the mountain so long that the Israelites thought he wasn't coming back.

They told Aaron, "Make us a golden calf to worship."

So Aaron asked them to bring him their gold rings and bracelets and from these he made a golden calf. He set it up in the camp and people started to pray to it. They forgot that God had brought them out of Egypt.

As Moses was coming down the mountain, he heard singing. He couldn't understand what the noise was about until he saw the calf of gold.

Moses was so angry that he smashed the stones with God's rules on them. He had to climb Mount Sinai all over again to get a new set. The Israelites told God they were sorry for making the golden calf.

God said the Israelites were to build a special tent, called the "tabernacle", where they could worship. It was easy to take it apart and carry it with them on their travels. They also made a golden box called the "ark of the covenant" for storing the Ten Commandments. It was kept inside the tent.

"Now continue your journey to the country I promised you," God told the Israelites. "I will be with you."

So the Israelites packed their tents, left Mount Sinai and moved on. They wandered through the desert for forty years.

Sometimes they grumbled and complained, but God never gave up on them.

After long years of wandering, Moses finally brought the Israelites to a mountain called Nebo. From the top they could see the land God had promised them.

But Moses died before he could enter the Promised Land.

Exodus 13–16, 19–20, 24–26, 32; Deuteronomy 34

Joshua destroys Jericho

At last the Israelites came to the River Jordan. On the other side lay the land God had promised them – the land of Canaan. But they had one more problem: how to cross the river.

God told the priests to walk into the water carrying the Holy Box containing God's laws. When they did so, God made a dry path. All the people followed. Then the waters of the river flooded back again.

Now the Israelites were in the Promised Land!

And they had a new leader, Joshua.

The first place they came to was the great city of Jericho. It had huge, thick walls, mighty gates, and guards posted everywhere.

The Israelites set up camp outside the walls of Jericho.

Then God told Joshua how to capture Jericho. "For six days, march the people around the city. On the seventh day, march around it seven times. Then the priests must blow a loud blast on their trumpets and everybody must shout. If you do all this, the walls of Jericho will fall and the city will be yours."

So the Israelites did as God had instructed.

On the seventh day, they marched around the great walls of Jericho seven times, following the priests and the Holy Box. The seventh time, the priests blew their trumpets and the Israelites shouted at the top of their voices.

Down crashed the walls of Jericho, as God had promised. Soon the Israelites had captured the whole city.

This was just the first of Joshua's many victories in Canaan. With Joshua leading them, the Israelites gradually took over the Promised Land.

Joshua 1–6

Samson the Strong

After Joshua died, the Israelites forgot about God and all that he had done for them. So God let the fierce Philistines attack their country.

One day, an angel told an Israelite named Manoah, "Your wife is going to have a baby. When he grows up, he will protect your people from the Philistines."

When the baby was born, his parents called him Samson. They never cut his hair – to show he had a special job to do.

When Samson grew up, he was extraordinarily strong. He killed a lion with his bare hands. He set fire to the Philistines' harvest standing ripe in the fields. He was unbeatable!

The Philistines were desperate to capture this super-strong man.

Then one day, Samson fell in love with a beautiful Philistine girl called Delilah.

The Philistine kings went to Delilah. "We'll give you more money than you can dream of," they told her, "if you can get Samson to tell you why he's so strong."

Delilah agreed at once! The next time she was with Samson, she asked slyly, "What is it that makes you so strong?"

But each time she asked, Samson told her something different.

"If you tie me up with new rope, I'll be as weak as anyone else," he said. Or, "Weave my hair into a loom and I'll be as weak as a baby." Delilah tried these out – but Samson was as strong as ever.

"If you don't tell me what makes you strong," Delilah moaned, "it shows you don't really love me."

So Samson gave in. "If someone shaves my head," he whispered, "I will lose all my strength."

As soon as Samson was snoring, Delilah cut off his hair. Snip, snip, snip!

Samson lost all his strength.

Philistine soldiers burst in, tied him up and dragged him off. No trouble at all!

Soon Samson was chained up in prison. But day by day his hair began to grow back. The Philistines didn't notice!

One night they threw a party for their god, Dagon.

"Let's get Samson from prison!" they said.

So they brought Samson to the temple where the party was being held. The Philistines jeered at Samson. "Aren't you supposed to be so strong?"

"Help me once more!" Samson prayed to God.

Samson pushed with all his might against the temple's pillars.

Down fell the roof on top of the partygoers. Every Philistine in the temple was killed. And so was Samson. This was his last great feat of strength.

Judges 13–16

Samuel listens to God

On the top of a hill stood God's tent. There lived the priests who taught the Israelites to love and obey God. Each year they held a great festival and crowds of people came to celebrate.

One year a man brought his wife, Hannah, to the festival. She longed to have a baby boy.

Eli, the chief priest, heard Hannah talking to God.

"Lord, let me have a son and I will give him to you, to help you," she prayed.

"Go home, Hannah," said Eli. "God has heard you."

Hannah went home happy. She felt sure she would have the son she wanted. And she did. "We will call our baby Samuel," she said when he was born. "I will give him to God, as I promised."

When Samuel had grown old enough, Hannah took him back to God's tent. Eli was waiting.

"Here is the child I asked for," Hannah said. "I have brought Samuel to help you serve God in his great tent."

Soon Samuel was able to help the priests with their jobs. Some of the priests taught him to read and write.

One night, while Samuel was asleep in bed, he heard a voice call, "Samuel! Samuel!"

He sat up startled.

He thought Eli was calling, and ran in to the old man.

"Here I am, Eli!" he said. "You called."
"I didn't, Samuel," said Eli. "Go and lie down again."
Samuel went back to his room and lay down.
But once more he heard a voice call, "Samuel!"

Samuel ran in to Eli, "Here I am again – you *did* call me."

The old priest said once more, "No, I didn't call you. Go back and lie down."

A third time the voice came, "Samuel! Samuel!"

And a third time Samuel went to Eli.

"Here I am, Eli: I'm *sure* I heard you call," he said.

By now Eli knew it must be God calling Samuel.

"Go and lie down, Samuel" said Eli. "If you hear the voice call again, say, 'Speak, Lord – your helper is listening.'"

Samuel felt a bit frightened when Eli said this. But he went back to his room.

He listened – and soon the voice came yet again, "Samuel! Samuel!"

This time Samuel answered, "Speak, Lord – your helper is listening!"

And God did speak to him. He told Samuel about some sad things that were going to happen.

When Samuel grew up, people said, "Truly he is a friend of God."

1 Samuel 1, 3

Israel in the Time of King David

Mediterranean Sea

PHOENICIA

Mount Gilboa

Lake Galilee

ISRAEL

River Jordan

Jericho

Jerusalem

Bethlehem

Dead Sea

Beersheba

PHILISTINES

JUDAH

David and the giant

One day God told Samuel, "You must find a new king to rule Israel."

A young shepherd boy named David lived with his family in the town of Bethlehem. David had seven grown-up brothers. He could sing beautifully and play brilliantly on the harp.

And David was a good shepherd too. He guarded his flock. He had a sling and used it to hurl stones at wild animals.

One day a lion and a bear came after David's sheep. He leapt up and killed the lion and then the bear.

God told Samuel, "Go to Bethlehem and find a man called Jesse. One of his sons will be the next king of Israel."

So Samuel went to Bethlehem, and Jesse paraded his seven grown-up sons before him.

But Samuel knew God hadn't chosen any of them, although they were handsome and strong. He was puzzled. "Are *all* your sons here?" he asked Jesse.

"All except David, my youngest – he's minding the sheep."
"Fetch him too," said Samuel.

As soon as David ran in, Samuel knew: *This is the boy God has chosen. When he is older, David will be next king of Israel.*

Soon Israel's enemies, the Philistines, came to do battle. David's brothers went to fight. One day David took some food to his brothers. As he talked to them, he saw a huge giant called Goliath march out from the Philistine camp.

"Who will fight me?" the giant bellowed. "Haven't you Israelites got *anyone* brave enough to face me?"

But the Israelites were scared of the terrible giant.

"I'll fight Goliath," said young David, bravely.

His brothers just laughed. So David went to King Saul. "I'm not afraid of the giant," he said. "I'll fight him for you."

But Saul said: "You're much too young!"

"God will help me," said David.

"Go then," said Saul and gave David his own sword.

"I can't even lift it," said David – and gave it back.

David went to the nearby brook, chose five smooth pebbles and tucked them in his shepherd's pouch.

Down the hill strode Goliath the mighty.

David went to meet the giant.

When the giant caught sight of David, he roared with laughter. But David put a pebble in his sling, whirled it around his head and let it fly.

The stone struck Goliath on his forehead and the giant dropped down.

When the Philistines saw their strongest man fall down dead, they all ran off. David had beaten the Philistines single-handed.

Years later, after King Saul died, David became king of Israel, just as Samuel had said he would.

I Samuel 16–17

The wisest of kings

David ruled as king of Israel for forty years. He won many battles against Israel's enemies.

David had many sons, and of these it was Solomon who became king when he died.

David gave his son Solomon this good advice: "Be a strong king. Trust God and obey his laws."

Solomon ruled Israel for many years. During his reign, the people of Israel lived in peace.

One night, soon after he became king, God spoke to Solomon in a dream.

"What gift would you most like from me?" he asked.

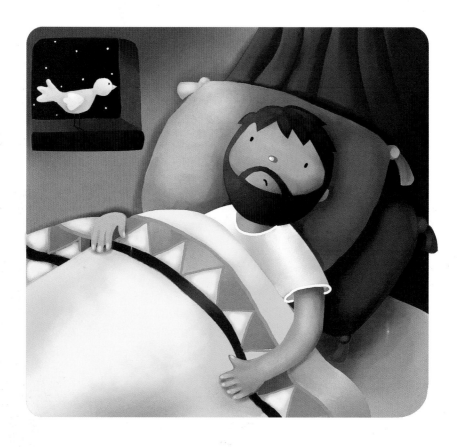

"Please, God, make me wise," replied King Solomon. "I want to make good choices when people ask what they should do."

God was pleased Solomon didn't ask for gold.

"I will make you wiser than anyone who has ever lived," God promised.

So it was that Solomon became the wisest of kings.

One day two women brought a baby to the palace. They showed King Solomon the baby.

"It's my baby," said one.

"No it's not – it's mine," shouted the other.

They were squabbling so noisily that Solomon had to cry, "*Silence!*"

The king needed to decide which woman was *really* the baby's mother. He thought hard, then said, "Call my captain of guards!"

When the captain arrived, Solomon ordered, "Take this baby and cut it exactly in two."

"No! No! – please don't do that!" one woman cried. "I'd rather *this* woman had the baby than it was cut in two."

Wise Solomon knew at once that she was the baby's mother. She had a true mother's love for her baby.

King Solomon built a wonderful temple where his people could worship God. His workmen used huge stones to construct the walls, and brought fine cedar wood to make the wall panels and furniture.

When the temple was finished, it was a wonderful sight. Inside was a room with no windows called the Holiest Place, where the

Holy Box was to be kept. The walls of this room were covered in gold.

In an outer room stood a gold altar and ten gold lampstands. Solomon made the temple as splendid as possible and put the very best furnishings inside it.

When everything was ready, Solomon held a special opening ceremony. The priests carried into the temple the Holy Box containing God's laws. At once the temple was filled with a dazzling light, to show God was with them. Afterwards, a great feast was held. It lasted a whole week!

1 Kings 2–3, 6–7

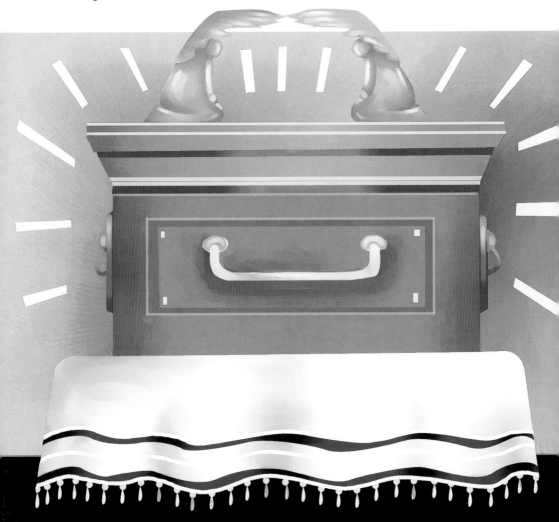

Elijah and the wicked king

After Solomon died, his kingdom split into two – the kingdoms of Israel and Judah. Both kingdoms were sometimes ruled by good kings, sometimes by bad.

King Ahab was one of the *very* bad kings of Israel. He married a wicked woman called Jezebel and did many things God said were wrong.

Elijah was one of God's special messengers, who the Bible calls "prophets". He told people what God thought about them.

God sent Elijah the prophet to teach Ahab a lesson.

"Ahab, king of Israel," said Elijah. "God says, because you have done so much wrong it will not rain in your kingdom for many years."

This made Ahab angry. King Ahab was *so* angry he wanted to harm Elijah.

So Elijah ran away to hide in the desert. There he lived alone beside a tiny stream. He drank its pure, flowing water.

But Elijah could find nothing to eat, away in the desert. He asked God to feed him.

So God sent Elijah big, black birds called ravens, carrying meat for him in their beaks. In this way, the prophet always had enough to eat.

But there was so little rain that one day the stream dried up. Now Elijah had nothing to drink. What was he to do now?

"I will show you where to find food and drink," God told him. "Start walking. On the road you will meet a woman. You must ask this woman to give you food."

Elijah set off just as God told him. And, as God had said, on the way he met a woman.

"Can you spare me some food?" Elijah asked politely.

"But I have only enough food for one last meal for me and my son," the woman told him.

"Cook something for me first," Elijah said to the woman. "If you do so, there will *still* be enough for you and for your son."

The woman did as he told her. She cooked a meal for Elijah and then prepared food for her son and herself.

Elijah stayed with the woman and her son.

And from that day the woman and her son never went without food.

After three whole years without rain, God spoke to Elijah: "Now go back and see King Ahab again."

So Elijah left the woman's house and went to the royal palace.

"It's you, is it, Elijah!" said the king. "How dare you come to my palace! You've brought nothing but trouble to my kingdom."

"*Rubbish!*" said Elijah. "It's you, Ahab, who has brought all the trouble to your kingdom. You have done so many wrong things that God has punished you and your people. It's *your* fault there's been no rain."

The king glowered. But in his heart he knew that Elijah was right.

"Now let's have a contest," Elijah went on. "Let's find out whose god is real – your god Baal or my God, the living God."

Ahab agreed. So they went to a hill called Mount Carmel to set things up for the competition.

Ahab's prophets ran around collecting stones to build an altar for their god Baal. And Elijah found just the right stones to build an altar for his God.

Then the contest began. The king's prophets placed offerings on their altar, then prayed for fire from heaven. They expected their god to send fire to burn up the sacrifice.
But nothing happened!

The king's prophets screamed at their god Baal – but no fire came.

Elijah teased them. "Pray louder!" he called. "Perhaps your god's asleep and can't hear."

They shouted even louder. But still nothing happened.

At last they gave up.

By now it was evening. Elijah placed an offering on his altar and poured water over it, to make it difficult to catch fire. Then he prayed, "God in heaven, send fire on my altar."

And fire came! It burned up the offering, the stones and even the water. Now the people of Israel knew that Elijah's God was the living God.

And God sent rain to Israel at last! After all the long, dry years.

But King Ahab and his horrible wife, Queen Jezebel, still wanted to have Elijah killed. He had to run away again to the desert. When he got there, he felt so tired he lay down and fell fast asleep.

Someone tapped Elijah on his shoulder. He looked up startled. Had Ahab's soldiers caught him? No – it was an angel who had come to feed him.

"Go and find a man named Elisha," said the angel. "He will help you – and continue your work after you've gone."

Elijah was no longer on his own. He was to have a helper.

1 Kings 16–19

After Elijah

Elijah set out to find his new helper. He discovered Elisha working in a field. Elijah put his cloak on the younger man to show he wanted Elisha to become his helper. Then Elisha said goodbye to his parents and followed Elijah.

Elijah was growing old, and Elisha went everywhere with him.

One day Elijah and Elisha were walking together. All of a sudden a flaming chariot and horses of fire appeared. The fiery horses drove the chariot between Elijah and Elisha. Then whoosh! Elijah went up to heaven in the chariot.

Elisha watched him go.

Then Elisha went on his way.

He met a woman who said, "I have nothing to eat – just this one little pot of oil."

"Collect up lots of empty pots and jars from your friends," Elisha said, "and pour your oil into them."

The woman collected up as many pots and jars as she could. Then she started pouring oil from her pot. It just kept coming! Soon she had filled every jar in the house.

Then the woman sold the oil, paid off all the money she owed, and bought food for her family.

Another woman came to ask Elisha for help.
"My little boy has died," she cried. "Please come and help me!"

Elisha went to her house and prayed for her son.
The little boy sneezed and opened his eyes.
He had come back to life!

Naaman, a great general in the army, had a horrible skin disease called leprosy. People with leprosy were not allowed to go near other people, in case they spread the disease.

Naaman's servant girl said, "I wish you could meet the prophet Elisha. He could heal you."

So Naaman went off in search of Elisha.

"Wash in the River Jordan seven times, and then you'll be well," Elisha told the general.

Naaman wasn't sure about this; it sounded a bit silly. But he decided to do what Elisha said. He went to the river to wash. And after the seventh time, the leprosy vanished!

2 Kings 2, 4, 5

Daniel, the king, and the lions

Darius the Great was king of the Medes and the Persians. He was a mighty king, with 120 governors to help rule his huge kingdom.

Daniel was one of Darius's governors. Daniel was so wise that Darius decided to make him chief governor of his kingdom.

Every morning, every lunchtime, and every night, Daniel prayed to God.

The other governors were jealous of Daniel. They tried to find some fault in him – but they couldn't.

So the jealous governors plotted against Daniel.

They went to the king. "O King Darius, live for ever," they said. "You only are wise and powerful." The king liked that!

"O king, make a new law," they continued. "A law that says no one must pray to anyone except you."

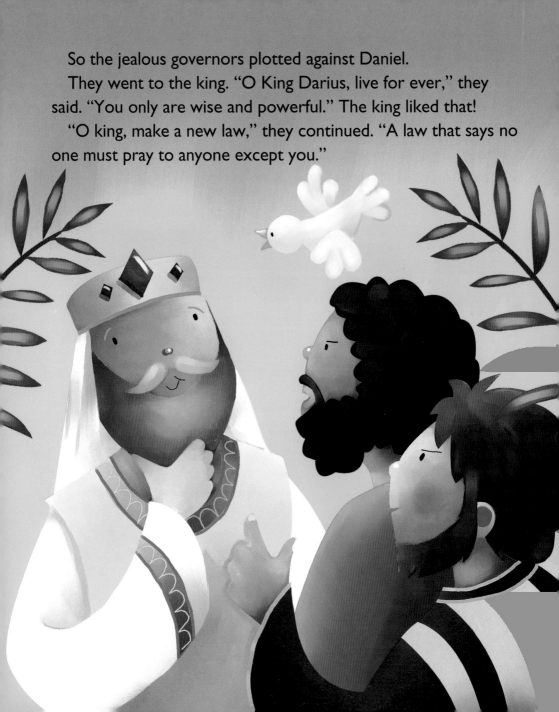

"If anyone disobeys this law," added one governor excitedly, "he'll be thrown into a pit full of lions."

The king puffed out his chest. This sounded great!

"Write out this new law for me," Darius told his governors.

The governors did so – and the king pressed his seal into the wax on the scroll they gave him. Now it was royal law.

The new law was proclaimed throughout the kingdom. "This is the law of the Medes and Persians; it cannot be changed."

Now the jealous governors hid where they could spy on Daniel's house. That very lunchtime they saw him go home and pray to God – just as he did every day.

The governors rushed straight back to King Darius.

"O king, live forever! Have you not ordered that nobody shall pray to any god except you?"

"Yes, of course I have!" said Darius.

"We've seen Daniel praying to his God," they said.

"Oh dear!" said Darius the Great. "Oh dear!"

Darius was sorry, because he liked Daniel. He tried to think of a way to save his top governor.

"The law of the Medes and Persians cannot be changed," the governors reminded him. "Daniel *must* be thrown into the lions' pit." So, sadly, the king agreed.

Soldiers seized Daniel, marched him to the pit of lions and locked him in.

That night the king wouldn't eat and couldn't sleep. He kept
thinking of poor Daniel in the pit of lions. As soon as morning
came, Darius leapt out of bed and hurried down to the lions' pit.
"Daniel!" he called. "Are you there? Are you all right?"

There stood Daniel – completely unharmed.

"O King!" said Daniel. "I'm here and I'm fine. There's not a scratch on me!"

"How come you're not hurt?" called Darius.

"God sent an angel to shut the mouths of the lions – so they couldn't bite me," Daniel told him.

Darius was overjoyed.

"Get Daniel out of this pit. Set him free at once!" shouted the king. "Go, arrest those wicked governors who trapped Daniel. From this day, everyone must respect Daniel's God. He is the living God... *This* is the law of the Medes and Persians. It cannot be changed."

Daniel 6

Jonah and the great big fish

One day God spoke to his prophet Jonah. "Go to the great city of Nineveh!" he said. "Tell the people there they are so bad that I'm going to punish them."

I don't want to go and tell these people God's going to punish them, Jonah thought. *It sounds much too scary!*

So he ran away instead.

Jonah went to the port and jumped on a ship going in the opposite direction. The ship sailed off, taking Jonah farther and farther away from the great city of Nineveh.

But before long God sent a mighty storm. The rain fell, lightning flashed and the waves rose higher and higher. The sea was soon so rough that the ship almost broke in half. The sailors were terrified!

"God, help us!" they cried out. "Don't let us drown!"

Jonah was sprawled out below deck, fast asleep. He hadn't even noticed the storm! The captain climbed down to find him.

"Wake up!" shouted the captain. "You need to help us!"

"God won't hear me," Jonah told him. "This is all my fault, because I disobeyed God. That's why he sent the storm."

But he went on deck with the captain.

"Throw me into the sea," Jonah yelled to the sailors. "Then perhaps the storm will stop and you'll be safe."

At first the sailors didn't want to do this. But the storm just kept getting wilder. So, with a great heave, the sailors tossed Jonah overboard and into the sea.

The moment Jonah hit the water, the storm stopped.
Down, down into the swirling water went Jonah. Then –
gulp! – something swallowed him whole. Now Jonah was in the
stomach of a massive fish that had been swimming past.

Jonah was in the tummy of that fish three whole days and three whole nights.

"Lord, save me!" he prayed. "Lord, save me!"

He was more scared now than when God had told him to go to Nineveh. And more scared than during the storm at sea.

But God heard Jonah pray. Before long the fish spat Jonah out onto the seashore. Jonah stood up, shook off the seaweed, dried himself and wondered what to do next.

Then God spoke to him again. "Jonah, go to the great city of Nineveh! Say to the bad people there: 'God is going to punish you.'"

This time Jonah did exactly what God told him.

He went to Nineveh and said to the people, "God is going to destroy your great city!"

The people of Nineveh were very frightened. "We're so sorry," they prayed. "Forgive us! We will change our ways."

God heard them. "I've decided not to destroy the city after all," he told the Ninevites.

So the ship was saved, Jonah was saved — and the city of Nineveh was saved too!

Jonah 1–3

New Testament

Roads to Bethlehem

The wise men may have come
by this route ∎ ∎ ∎ ∎ ∎ ∎ ∎

The likely route of Mary and
Joseph to Bethlehem ∎ ∎ ∎ ∎

Mount Hermon

GALILEE

Lake Galilee

Mediterranean
Sea

Nazareth

River Jordan

JUDEA

Jerusalem

Bethlehem

Dead Sea

Jesus is born

There was a young woman called Mary, who lived in the little town of Nazareth. One day an angel appeared to her. His name was Gabriel.

"Greetings, Mary!" the angel said. "I have wonderful news! God has a very important job for you."

Mary was amazed – and a bit frightened.

"You're going to have a baby," said the angel. "You must call him Jesus. God has sent him to save the world."

"How can this happen? I'm not even married yet."

Mary could hardly believe what she was hearing.

"With God nothing is impossible." said the angel.

Mary overflowed with happiness. "I will do whatever God wants," she said.

Mary loved the village carpenter, a man called Joseph. He was a kind, good man. Soon after Gabriel's visit, Joseph had a dream. In the dream, an angel told him, "Joseph, you need to look after Mary."

So Mary and Joseph got married straight away.

It was nearly time for Mary's baby to be born. Then one day soldiers nailed up a notice. It said, "Everyone must return to the town where they were born, and register their name."

So Joseph and Mary had to go back to Joseph's home town, Bethlehem.

Mary and Joseph set out on the long journey. They slept where they could, wrapped in their warm coats.

"Are we nearly there?" said Mary. "I'm so tired."

"Look – there are the lights of Bethlehem," said Joseph. "We'll soon be there."

"How will we find anywhere to stay?" asked Mary. "There are so many people here."

Joseph knocked on the door of an inn.

"Do you have a room?" asked Joseph.

The innkeeper shook his head. "No, I'm sorry. We're completely full!"

Then the innkeeper caught sight of Mary's tired face.
"There's a little stable where the animals sleep," he said.
"You're welcome to use that!"
They went to the stable and Mary lay down in the straw.
There, among the donkeys and cows, Mary's baby was born.

Mary wrapped baby Jesus in a long piece of cloth.
"Joseph – we don't have a cradle for our baby," she said.
So Joseph placed clean straw in the animals' feed box.
"I've made a bed," said Joseph and put the child gently in the manger. Baby Jesus fell asleep in the straw.

Luke 1, 2

The shepherds' story

It was dark in the fields outside Bethlehem. But the shepherds were still awake, making sure their sheep were safe.

Suddenly the sky became bright.

"What's that light?" asked one shepherd.

They were all really scared.

"It's an angel!" said another shepherd, very frightened.

"Don't be afraid," said the angel. "I have good news that will bring joy to everyone. Today your king has been born in Bethlehem. You'll find him lying in a manger. Go and see for yourselves!"

The shepherds listened in wonder.

Then a crowd of angels filled the sky, singing, "Glory to God on high – and peace to his people on earth!"

The light faded and the night became quiet again.

"We've seen angels!" said the first shepherd.

"You heard what the angel said – a king has been born," said another. "Tonight – here in Bethlehem!"

"Come on!"

And they rushed off into Bethlehem to find the baby king.
Soon the shepherds found the stable.

They peered in and saw Mary, Joseph, and baby Jesus lying in a manger. They all crowded in.

Then the shepherds knelt before baby Jesus.

They told Mary and Joseph what the angel had said to them. Everyone was astonished.

Then, noticing Mary was tired, the shepherds went back to their sheep.

But Mary kept thinking over what they had said.

Luke 2

The wise men's story

At the time Jesus was born, some wise men in a distant country were looking at the stars.

"Look!" said one. "A special star has come up in the east."
They searched their books to find out what it might mean.
"It shows that a new king is born," said another.

So the wise men decided to set out to find the newborn king. They crossed the desert on their camels. The star led them many, many miles.

The wise men followed the special star all the way to the city of Jerusalem. They went to the palace of King Herod.

"Where is the child who is to be king of the Jews?" they asked.

"What new king?" King Herod asked.

He knew nothing about all this, so he summoned his advisers.

"Where will this new king be born?" Herod asked them.

"In the town of Bethlehem," they said. "That's what is written in our Scriptures."

Then Herod sent for the visitors.

"My advisers say you'll find the new king in Bethlehem," he said. "Go and find him. Please come back and tell me, so I can go and worship him too."

But Herod didn't really want to go and *worship* the newborn king – he wanted to *kill* him!

At last the star led the wise men to Bethlehem. There it stopped, right over the place where Jesus was.

The wise men bowed down before baby Jesus. They had found the king! They gave him their gifts: gold, and rich perfumes called frankincense and myrrh.

But that night, as they slept, an angel appeared to the wise men. "Don't return to King Herod's palace," said the angel. "He wants to kill the baby! Go back to your own land – but take a different road."

In the morning, the wise men left Bethlehem and went home a different way.

God sent an angel to Joseph in a dream again.

"Take baby Jesus and Mary and flee to Egypt," the angel said. "King Herod wants to harm Jesus. Stay in Egypt until it's safe to go home."

It was still night, but Joseph woke Mary and Jesus and they left hurriedly. They set off through the darkness to Egypt, where they stayed, safe from wicked King Herod.

Matthew 2

Jesus lost in Jerusalem

Mary and Joseph stayed in Egypt with Jesus until they heard it was safe to return home. Then they set out on the long journey back to Nazareth, where they lived. At last they saw the little houses of Nazareth, nestled among the hills.

Jesus grew up in Nazareth. Joseph worked as a carpenter and Jesus often helped him in his workshop. Sometimes Jesus played with other children. Sometimes he helped the shepherds with their sheep. And sometimes he watched the women fetch water from the well.

When he was old enough, Jesus went to school. The teacher helped him to learn to read. Jesus listened carefully to the lessons and remembered everything he was taught. He also learned about God's laws.

Once a year the Jewish people had a great festival. They loved to go to Jerusalem, where the great temple stood.

When Jesus was twelve years old, Mary said, "This year you can come with us to the festival in Jerusalem. You're old enough now to know the law of God. It's time you came to the temple with us."

It was an exciting journey over the hills to Jerusalem. At last they were approaching the city. From the hills around they could see the great temple gleaming in the sun.

Mary, Joseph, and Jesus immediately went to the temple. *This is the house of God, my heavenly father*, thought Jesus.

In the temple he met with wise men and priests.

Soon the great festival was over and it was time to go home.

They started on the journey back to Nazareth. Mary didn't see Jesus all that day.

"We need to look for him," said Mary anxiously.

Nobody had seen Jesus since they left Jerusalem.

"We'll have to go back," said Joseph.

But they couldn't find Jesus in the busy streets of Jerusalem. "There's only one place left to look –" said Mary "the temple itself. Jesus loved being in the temple. Perhaps he went back."

And, sure enough, there they found Jesus. He'd been in the temple all the time. He'd found the wise men again and was asking them questions. They were astonished that such a young boy knew so much about the law of God.

Jesus saw his parents looking at him, Mary almost in tears.

"Jesus, my son!" she said. "Why did you do this? We've been so worried."

"Didn't you know where I'd be?" he asked, surprised. "I had to come to my father's house."

Then Jesus set off home with Mary and Joseph. He often thought of what he learned during those days with the wise men in the temple.

Luke 2

John baptizes Jesus

John was Jesus' cousin. He was different from other people. He lived in the desert. He wore rough clothes made of camel's hair tied up with a leather belt. And he lived on food he found in the desert – wild honey and grasshoppers called locusts.

God had given John a special job to do – preaching.

"You do a lot of bad things," John told people. "Turn around and start doing what's right."

Some people asked, "How should we make a fresh start?"

"If you've got two shirts," he said, "give one to somebody who doesn't have any shirts," or, "If you've got enough to eat, share with someone who's hungry."

People were shocked when he said this sort of thing.

Crowds of people flocked to hear John.

"God wants to forgive you when you've gone wrong," he told them. Many said they were sorry for wrong things they'd done. John baptized them in the River Jordan. He dipped them under the water. This showed they wanted to begin a new way of living. People called him "John the Baptizer" or "John the Baptist".

One day some people came to John. "Are you the special one God is sending to save us?" they asked.

"Before long, someone much greater than me will come," John replied. "I'm not worthy even to undo his sandals!"

Soon after, Jesus came to John beside the River Jordan.
"Baptize me," Jesus said to John. "It's what God wants."
"But Jesus, I should be baptized by you," said John.
"This is the way God wants it," Jesus replied.

So John dipped Jesus in the River Jordan.

When Jesus came up out of the water, a dove appeared above his head.

And a voice from heaven said, "This is my own dear son. I am very pleased with him."

Matthew 3

Jesus chooses his team

One day Jesus was standing beside Lake Galilee. He was telling the people stories and talking about God's law.

Lots of people crowded around him, listening.

Jesus noticed two empty fishing boats on the beach. The fishermen were busy washing their nets.

Jesus climbed into one of the boats, the one owned by Simon Peter. Jesus asked him to push it out a little way from the shore.

Then Jesus spoke to the people from the boat.

When Jesus had finished teaching the crowd, he said to Simon Peter, "Now push out into deep water and let down your nets so you can catch plenty of fish."

"Master," answered Simon Peter, "we've been hard at work all night and not caught a single fish. However, if you say so, we'll let down the nets again."

The fishermen let down their nets once more.

This time their nets were so full of fish that they began to tear. Simon Peter and his brother Andrew called to their friends in the other boat to help them.

Soon both boats were so full of fish that they nearly sank.

Simon Peter and Andrew and their fishermen friends, the brothers James and John, were amazed to see so many fish.

Simon Peter knelt before Jesus. "Leave me, Lord – I am a bad man," he said. But Jesus said to him, "From now on you're going to be fishing for people."

So the fishermen left their boats and followed Jesus. They became some of Jesus' special friends, his disciples.

Tax collectors weren't much liked. They swindled people and took too much money.

One day Jesus saw a taxman called Matthew working at his desk.

"Follow me," Jesus called over to him.

At once Matthew got up, left his money, and followed Jesus.

Jesus called some more men to be his special friends.

Philip, Bartholomew, Thomas the twin, another James, Thaddaeus, Simon the Zealot, and Judas Iscariot.

There were twelve altogether. They became Jesus' disciples.

Luke 5, 6

Jesus teaches on a hill

Jesus often climbed the hills around Galilee. One day, a crowd gathered to listen to him on a hill.

Jesus taught them about the blessings God gives.

"God blesses those people who are humble.
The earth will belong to them!
    "God blesses those people whose hearts are pure.
They will see him!

"You are the salt for everyone on earth. But if salt no longer tastes like salt, how can it make food salty?

"You are the light for the whole world.

"Love your enemies and pray for anyone who mistreats you. Then you will be acting like your Father in heaven."

Then Jesus taught his followers about prayer.

"Go somewhere quiet when you want to pray to God," he said. "God knows exactly what you need. And this is how you should pray to him:

Our Father in heaven,
May your holy name be kept holy;
May your kingdom come;
May your will be done on earth, as it is in heaven.
Give us today the food we need.
Forgive us the wrongs we have done,
As we forgive the wrongs that others have done to us.
Do not bring us to hard testing,
But keep us safe from evil.

"Don't store up money and buy things here on earth that can be taken from you. Instead, store up riches in heaven, where God will give you everything you need," said Jesus.

"Don't worry where your next meal is coming from. Look at the birds in the air. They don't sow seeds or gather a harvest, but God cares for them. You are far more important to him than they are.

"Don't worry about what you're going to wear. Look how God clothes the flowers in the fields. They don't work, but God takes care of them.

"Trust God and he will provide you with all these things."

Matthew 5–6

The boy who left home

"Jesus has some strange friends," people said. "He often eats with bad people."

Jesus heard them and felt sad. Didn't they know that God loves people even when they do wrong? So Jesus told them this story:

There was once a very rich farmer. He had a beautiful house, a huge farm, many servants, great flocks of sheep and a big herd of cows. And best of all he had two sons.

Dad has lots of money, the younger son thought one day. *But I won't get my share until he dies. I'll ask him for my share now.*

So he went to his father. "Dad," he said. "You have lots of money. I don't want to wait to get my share. Give me my money now, and I can go off and enjoy myself."

The father felt sad. He loved having his son at home. But he gave the younger son his share of the money.

That same day the boy packed his bags and left home.

His dad was very sorry to see his son leave. Each morning he would climb onto the roof of his house to see if the boy might be coming home.

But the younger son kept walking until he reached a distant city. There he bought himself a house and gave lots of parties. It was great! He could eat and drink with his new friends from morning until night. He had a wonderful time!

But one day the money ran out – and when the money went, the boy's new friends disappeared too. No more parties! No friends! No work! No money!

I must find some work and earn some money, he thought. *I'll starve if I can't buy any food.*

But it was difficult to get work. And to make it worse, famine came and there was little food for anyone. So the boy went to see a farmer.

"I'm starving," he told the farmer. "Give me a job and I'll work hard for you."

"Look after my herd of pigs," said the farmer.

So the boy sat minding the grunting, greedy pigs.

I'm so hungry I could eat the pigs' food, the boy thought to himself one day. Then he remembered his family at home.

How stupid I am! he thought. *The men working for my father get all the food they need. I know what I'll do! I'll go home and say, "Father, I've done wrong in God's sight — and in yours too. I don't deserve to be called your son any more. But can I work for you and earn enough to pay for my meals?"*

So the boy set off home. He was dirty and tired and his clothes were in rags. But his father had never forgotten him. This day, as usual, his father was watching from the roof.

Far in the distance he spied a tiny figure. Could it be his dear, lost son?

"It *is* my son," said the old man.

And while the boy was still a long way off, his happy father ran to meet him. He hugged and kissed his son.

The boy started the speech he'd been practising.

"Dad, I'm so sorry… I don't deserve to be called your son… Can I work as your servant?…"

But his father started laughing.

"My son has come home!" he shouted. "Quick – bring the best clothes we have and put them on him. Put a gold ring on his finger. Cook a banquet! I thought my son was dead, but he's back home. He was lost – now he's found. We'll have such a party!"

Luke 15

The lost sheep

Jesus told another great story.

There was once a good shepherd. He had exactly 100 sheep. He knew them all by name. He loved every single one of them.

Each morning the shepherd counted his sheep. One, two, three, four… 97, 98, 99, 100.

Each day the shepherd took his sheep to grassy green fields. He found them a stream to drink from. He guarded his flock and scared off wild animals.

Each night the shepherd led his sheep back to the fold. He counted them in again. One, two, three, four… 97, 98, 99, 100. The whole flock was safe!

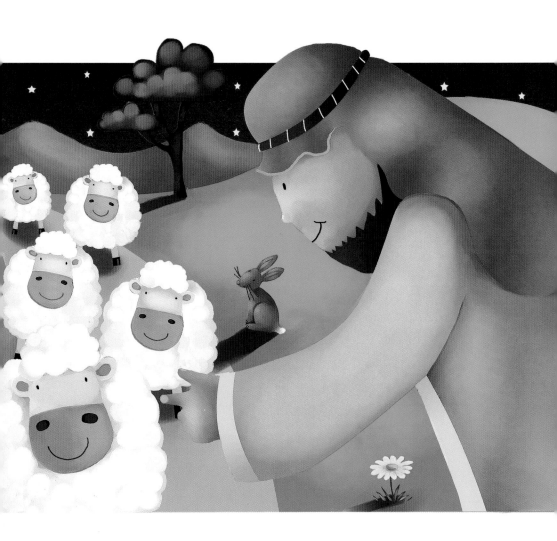

One night the shepherd was counting his sheep as usual. One, two, three, four… 97, 98, 99 – only 99!

Oh no! He must have missed one.

The shepherd counted again. One, two, three, four… 97, 98, 99… One sheep was definitely missing. Now he was worried.

"I must go and find the missing sheep," said the shepherd.

So the shepherd took his stick and set out to search for his lost sheep. He splashed across a stream and clambered over rocks. He climbed a hill and stumbled down the other side. But the shepherd saw no sheep.

"Where are you?" he called.

The shepherd walked for miles. It was dark and cold and he was tired and hungry. He searched all the places where the sheep might have strayed. He heard a wolf howl.

The shepherd stopped and listened.

"Baa!"

The shepherd listened again. It must be the lost sheep!

The shepherd pulled his sheep from the bush where it had got caught. Its woolly coat was torn.

At last the shepherd had found the lost sheep.

The shepherd carried the sheep home gently on his shoulders. How happy he was! He called his friends together. "Let's celebrate!" he said. "I've found my lost sheep!"

Jesus said, "I am like the good shepherd. I too care for people who are lost."

Luke 15

The stranger who helped

Once a man asked Jesus, "What must I do to please God?"

"You're a religious sort of person," replied Jesus. "What does the Bible say?"

The man answered, "Love God and love other people!"

"Then do just that!" said Jesus.

But then the man asked: "Which people?"

So Jesus told this story:

There was once a man who was walking from Jerusalem to Jericho. Suddenly there was a shout. Before the man knew what was happening, robbers leapt out from behind the rocks. They stole everything he had and left him lying on the ground.

The man lay on the road. His head was aching. What was he to do? Then he heard *flip-flop, flip-flop*. It was a priest walking to Jerusalem.

"Help!" the man called out feebly.

But the priest crossed to the other side of the road and walked on. The *flip-flop* of his sandals gradually disappeared.

The injured man lay still again. Then he heard the *clomp-clomp*, *clomp-clomp* of boots. It was someone else on the Jerusalem road. This time it was a helper from the temple.

The man called out again, "Help! Help!"

But the temple-helper crossed over and started to walk faster! Straight past the poor, injured man.

By now the sun was sinking. The man lay still. Then he heard the *clip-clop, clip-clop* of a donkey. But the injured man saw it was a Samaritan, a foreigner from Samaria. The Samaritans were fierce enemies.

But when the Samaritan reached the man, he shouted "Whoa!" to his donkey and walked over.

"What's happened here?" he asked kindly.

"Robbers beat me and took everything," said the man.
The Samaritan poured oil on his wounds and bandaged them.
Then he helped the injured man climb onto his donkey.

By now it was getting dark.

Moving slowly, at last they reached a house. The Samaritan lifted down the injured man.

"Do you have a room for this poor man?" he called. "Please look after him and make sure he has all the food and medicine he needs. I'll pay for everything!"

They put him to bed – and by morning he was feeling much better.

"Now," asked Jesus, "which of the three men – the priest, the temple-helper or the Samaritan – acted like a good friend to the man who was robbed?"

"The man who helped."

"Go and do the same," said Jesus.

Luke 10

The two house builders

Jesus told the people another story.

Once two men each decided to build a house.

The first man soon found a sandy place, with a stream gurgling past. "This is a great place to build!" he said.

So he started to build his house on the sand.

This man was in such a hurry that he didn't dig any foundations.

His house was soon finished.

The second man searched hard for the best place to build his house. At last he found some solid rock. He dug into the rock. It was tiring work. Then this man started to build the walls of his house.

The walls of the house grew tall. The man added a neat red roof and a chimney.

Finally it was all finished.

Almost at once black clouds appeared. Rain fell, winds blew, lightning flashed and thunder roared.

The two men both rushed into their houses.

Then CRRRAASHH!!! The first man's house fell flat!

The man who built on the sand was left with – nothing!

But despite the storm, the second man's house stood firm.
Jesus said, "People who listen to what God says are like the
wise man who built his house on rock."

Luke 6

How many times?

"How many times should I forgive someone who has wronged me?" Simon Peter asked Jesus one day. "Seven times?"

"No," said Jesus, "not seven – but seventy times seven."

Then Jesus told his followers this story:

Once there was a great and good king.
He lent some money to his servants.

The day came for the money to be paid back. But one servant owed the king so much he couldn't possibly pay it back.

The king was angry and ordered the man and his family to be sold to get back the money. But the man pleaded with the king to give him more time to pay, as he had served him well for years.

"You're right," said the king. "You have served me well." And he rubbed out everything the man owed him.

That same day the servant met a man who owed *him* a little money. He grabbed the man. "Pay up – or I'll have you thrown into prison," he shouted. The man pleaded with him for more time to pay, but the servant wouldn't listen.

When the king heard about this, he called for his servant.

"I forgave you a great deal — but you would not forgive this man a little. Now you must go to prison until you pay back *everything* you owe me."

Jesus turned to Simon Peter (who he named Peter).

"That is how God will treat you if you do not forgive other people," he said.

Matthew 18

Jesus in Galilee

Mediterranean
Sea

PHOENICIA

Capernaum

Bethsaida

Cana

GALILEE

Lake
Galilee

Nazareth

River Jordan

The boy with loaves and fishes

One day a little boy who lived near Lake Galilee saw lots of people on the hills.

"Why have you all come here?" he asked.

"We're looking for Jesus," said a woman. "He sailed across the lake with his friends."

"Who's Jesus?" asked the little boy.

"Don't you know?" a girl asked him. "He does miracles and tells great stories."

"I wish I could hear some of them," said the boy. "I'll go and ask if I can come."

So he ran home. "Mother!" panted the boy. "Can I go and hear Jesus' stories?"

"Of course you can!" said his mother. "I'll pack some food for you. Look, here are five little loaves and two fish."

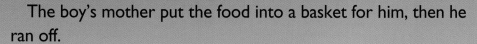

The boy's mother put the food into a basket for him, then he
ran off.

"Is Jesus here yet?" he asked when he arrived.

"He's over there," said a man, "with his friends."

Jesus had come to the hills for a rest, but when he saw the
crowds of people, he felt sorry for them.

Jesus' friends were walking among the crowd, looking for sick people to take to Jesus. The boy saw Jesus put his hands on people who were ill and talk to them. Suddenly they were well. They could see, they could walk and run again! They went away, thanking God.

Then Jesus sat down and started telling the people some of his wonderful stories. The boy listened carefully so he wouldn't miss a word.

The day went on and soon the sun began to set. Thousands of people were on the hills, excited and happy. But they were beginning to feel a bit tired. And hungry.

"Master," said one of Jesus' friends. "Shall we send these people away to buy bread?"

"No – we must feed them here," said Jesus. "Has anyone got some food?"

Jesus' friends went around the hillside asking, "Has anyone brought food with them?" Everyone shook their heads.

Then the little boy heard them. He looked at his five little loaves and two small fish.

I would love to give them to Jesus, he thought.

So the boy went to one of Jesus' friends.

"I have a little bread," he said, "and two small fish. Jesus can have them."

The disciple took the boy to Jesus.

"Master," he said, "here's a boy with five loaves and two fish."

Jesus smiled at the boy and took his basket.

"Tell everyone to sit down in groups," Jesus told his friends.

Then Jesus took the loaves and broke them. He thanked God, then gave some to his friends. Next Jesus divided the fish.

Jesus' friends started to give the food to the crowds on the hillside.

To the little boy's amazement, Jesus always had more. He went on breaking up the bread and fish.

There seems to be no end to my bread and fishes! thought the boy. *How can so little become so much? Jesus must be doing one of his miracles!*

More than 5,000 people were sitting on the hillside – and every one of them had enough to eat.

When they had all eaten as much as they wanted, Jesus asked his friends to pick up the leftovers.

The little boy counted. "Twelve baskets full of scraps," he said. "And I brought one little basket of food. This is a *really* great miracle!"

John 6

Jesus helps a little girl

There was a little girl who lived in the village of Capernaum. Her father was called Jairus. One day she woke up feeling ill. The doctor came to see her, but the girl was no better. Her parents were very worried. "Have you heard of this healer, Jesus?" Jairus asked his wife. "He's staying here in Capernaum."

"Go and find him," said his wife. "See if he'll come and help our daughter."

287

Jairus rushed off into the town. Anxiously he asked people where he would find Jesus. He went to the house where Jesus usually stayed – but he wasn't there.

"Go to the lake," said the woman who opened the door. "He might be teaching there."

So Jairus hurried to the lakeside, where he saw a crowd of people.

"Is Jesus here?" asked Jairus.

"No," said a fisherman.

But someone shouted, "Look, I can see a boat now. Jesus is coming!"

Minutes later the boat ran up onto the shore. Jesus jumped out.

Jairus begged Jesus to come and see his little girl.

"She's terribly ill," said Jairus, his voice a bit wobbly.

Jesus saw how worried Jairus looked. "I'll come at once," he said.

But just then a messenger rushed up. "Jairus," he said. "Don't bother Jesus now. Your little girl is dead."

"Don't be afraid," Jesus said gently to Jairus. "Just believe!"

Jesus walked on with Jairus, and the crowd followed. When they were near Jairus's house, Jesus said to the crowd, "Don't come any further."

Then, taking just his special friends James, Peter, and John, Jesus went into Jairus's house.

As soon as they were inside, they heard lots of weeping and wailing.

"Please go away!" said Jesus to the people making all the noise. "The little girl isn't dead – she's sleeping."

They laughed at him. But Jesus sent them off anyway, and followed Jairus into the room where the little girl lay.

The girl's mother stood there. "You're too late, Jairus," she sobbed.

Jesus took the little girl's hand gently in his warm hands.

"My dear, get up!" he said.

The little girl opened her eyes. Then she sat up and looked around. She smiled at her father.

The girl's father and mother kissed and hugged her, crying for joy.

"Find your dear daughter something to eat," said Jesus.

Once she'd had some food and a drink, she felt much better.

Luke 8

Jesus and the storm

Jesus was with his special friends, the disciples, beside Lake Galilee. Many people had come to listen to him telling his wonderful stories.

When evening came, Jesus said to his friends, "Come on, let's go across to the other side of the lake."

So they said goodbye to the people who'd been listening, climbed into their boat, and set off across the lake.

Jesus felt very tired. He had been talking to crowds of people all day and needed a rest. Jesus lay his head on a pillow and went to sleep.

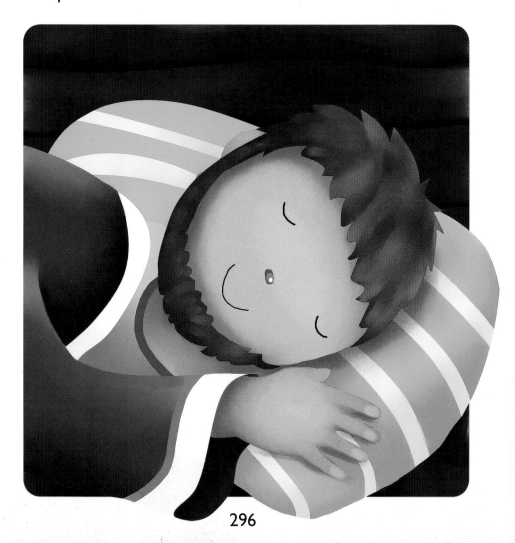

Suddenly, a fierce wind blew from the hills surrounding the lake. Rain fell. High waves splashed all around. The boat was tossed to and fro. It began to rock dangerously and fill with water. The disciples were very frightened.

But Jesus was still sleeping peacefully. The disciples decided to wake him.

"Master, wake up!" they shouted. "Do something to save us — or we're all going to drown!"

Jesus awoke and stood up.

"Be still!" he said to the wind and waves.

At that very moment the wind dropped. The waves ceased.
Everything was still. The waters of the lake lay silent around
them.

Jesus turned to his disciples, "Why were you so frightened?"
he asked. "I am with you. You can always trust me."

"Where does Jesus get such astonishing power?" the friends asked
each other. "Even the wind and the waves do what he tells them!"

Luke 8

Palestine in Jesus' Time

Most of Jesus' teaching took place in the region of Galilee

Mediterranean Sea

GALILEE

Capernaum

Lake Galilee

Nazareth

 SAMARIA

River Jordan

JUDEA

Jericho

Jerusalem

Bethlehem

Dead Sea

Jesus and the crippled man

Jesus was teaching inside a house. Many people had come, wanting to see Jesus, and the building was full. No one else could get in.

Then four men came along carrying a sick friend. He couldn't walk. They wanted to bring him to Jesus.

As the men couldn't get inside the house, they climbed onto the roof. They tore a big hole in the roof and let down their sick friend on his mattress.

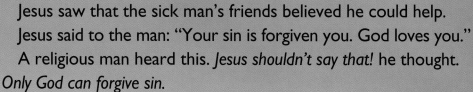

Jesus saw that the sick man's friends believed he could help.
Jesus said to the man: "Your sin is forgiven you. God loves you."
A religious man heard this. *Jesus shouldn't say that!* he thought.
Only God can forgive sin.

Jesus knew what the man was thinking. "Which is easier?"
he asked. "To say to this sick man: 'your sin is forgiven' or
to make him well? I wanted to show that I can forgive sin."

Then Jesus said to the paralyzed man: "Stand up! Pick up your mattress and go home."

That moment, the man got up. He picked up his mattress and walked out of the house. People watching were astonished. "We've never seen anything like it!" they said.

Luke 5

Jesus comes to Zacchaeus

Zacchaeus lived in Jericho. He was a tax collector and took much more money than he was supposed to. Everyone disliked him.

"Zacchaeus is only rich because he takes lots of our money," they said.

One day Zacchaeus heard that Jesus was visiting Jericho. He really wanted to see Jesus – but he was very short. People would stand in his way.

So Zacchaeus ran ahead of the crowds and climbed a tree. Now he *would* see Jesus when he passed by.

When Jesus came along, he stopped by the tree. He had seen Zacchaeus up in its branches.

Jesus called out: "Zacchaeus, come down! I want to visit your home today!"

Zacchaeus slid down the tree and took Jesus home for a meal.
He was very happy that Jesus had come to visit him.

But the people were annoyed.

They started to complain: "Zacchaeus is a bad man. Jesus shouldn't be going to see such a horrible person!"

But Zacchaeus told Jesus: "I've taken too much money from people. I want to put things right. I'm going to give back all the money I stole from people – *and* I'm going to give half my money to the poor!"

Jesus said, "Today is a special day for you, Zacchaeus. God is happy with you. Anyone can come to God – like you have – and make a new start."

Luke 19

Jesus visits Mary and Martha

Jesus visited the village of Bethany, where there lived two sisters, named Mary and Martha. The sisters were very different from each other.

Martha invited Jesus to their home.

Then Mary sat down while Jesus talked to her about God's kingdom. She listened carefully.

But Martha wanted to prepare a great meal for Jesus and was very busy in the kitchen. She started thinking, *Why isn't Mary helping me?*

Soon she felt quite cross, so she went to Jesus and said, "Lord, can't you see: I'm doing all the work on my own. Here's Mary sitting doing *nothing*. Tell her to help me!"

But Jesus answered, "Martha, you're worrying too much about unimportant things and forgetting what's *really* important. Mary is doing the right thing: she's listening to me. What Mary is learning from me can never be taken away from her."

Mary and Martha had a brother called Lazarus. One day he fell ill. Mary and Martha sent a message to Jesus asking him to come and heal their brother.

Jesus loved his three friends, yet he waited a couple of days before setting out to see them. And before Jesus arrived, Lazarus had died.

Martha and Mary felt very upset.

"If you'd come earlier," they told Jesus, "our brother wouldn't have died."

Jesus was sad too. He cried.

Then Jesus went to the tomb of Lazarus. "Lazarus, come out!" he called. And out came Lazarus, still wrapped in the special burial cloths. He was alive and well!

How happy were his sisters, Mary, and Martha! Everyone watching was amazed.

Luke 10, John 11

316

Jesus rides into Jerusalem

It was time for the Jewish festival of Passover. Jesus decided to go to Jerusalem for the festival with his special friends, the twelve disciples.

On the way Jesus told them, "I'm going to be taken prisoner and killed in Jerusalem. But after three days, I will be raised from the dead."

But they didn't understand what he meant.

When they were approaching the village of Bethany, just outside Jerusalem, Jesus sent off two of his friends.

"Go to the next village," he told them. "You'll find a donkey there. Untie it and bring it to me. If anyone asks what you're doing, just say, 'The Master needs the donkey!'"

The disciples found the donkey and brought it to Jesus. Some of them spread their cloaks over its back. Then Jesus sat on the donkey and rode into Jerusalem. When the crowds saw him coming, they grew excited. Many welcomed Jesus as king, spreading their cloaks on the ground before him. Others cut branches from palm trees and threw them on the road. Soon everyone was chanting, "*Hosanna!* Hooray for God!"

But some of the priests hated Jesus and were plotting to kill him. One of Jesus' disciples, Judas Iscariot, went to the priests.

"If you pay me well," he said, "I will show you where to find Jesus and arrest him."

The priests were delighted. They promised to pay Judas, so he waited for a good moment to hand Jesus over to them.

When they arrived in Jerusalem, Jesus and his followers went to the temple.

Jesus saw that shopkeepers had set up tables and were selling things and changing money.

Jesus was very angry.

"You've turned God's temple into a den of thieves!" he shouted.

Then Jesus chased them right out of the temple, throwing over their tables and overturning their stalls.

"My temple should be a place of prayer," he said.

Luke 19

A special meal with Jesus

The day arrived for the feast of Passover itself. At Passover, Jewish people cook lamb for dinner in their homes.

Jesus wanted to celebrate it with his twelve special friends, the disciples.

They ate this special supper in an upstairs room in Jerusalem.

As they sat together Jesus said, "Love one another, just as I have loved you." Then he added, "One of you eating with me is going to hand me over to my enemies."

The disciples were scared. "Jesus, you can't mean me!" said one.

Jesus said, "It's someone dipping into the same bowl of food as I am."

Just then Judas crept out. He had been plotting against Jesus.

Jesus took some bread. He thanked God for it, broke it and gave a piece to each of his friends. "Take this and eat it!" Jesus said. "I am the bread. I am giving myself for you all."

Then Jesus took a cup of wine and thanked God for it.

He passed the cup to his disciples, saying, "Drink this wine! The wine is my life. I offer my life for all."

When everyone had finished, they sang a hymn.

After supper, Jesus took his disciples outside the city to a garden called Gethsemane. "Wait here for me," he said. "I want to pray. Stay awake and pray too."

Jesus chose three of his friends – Peter, James, and John – to pray with him.

"I'm so sad," he told them. "Please stay here and pray."

Jesus went a little further. Then he prayed, "Father, don't let me have to do this… But it's not what I want, it's what you want that should be done."

He walked back and found all the disciples fast asleep.

"Peter," Jesus said, waking him. "Couldn't you pray with me for just an hour? Keep watch and pray."

He went off alone again. But the disciples fell asleep once more.

Later, Jesus came back. "Wake up!" he said. "Here's the man who's going to betray me."

And there was Judas, with some men brandishing swords and sticks. Judas had told them, "The man I kiss is the one you must arrest." He walked up to Jesus and kissed him, so the soldiers grabbed Jesus and took him prisoner.

The disciples ran off, leaving Jesus all alone.

John 13, 18

The first Easter

The soldiers marched Jesus off to the high priest, who called together the other priests.

"Are you the king who God has sent?" the high priest asked Jesus. "Are you the Son of God?"

"Yes," Jesus answered, "I am."

"Did you hear him?" the priests shouted angrily. "He says he's the Son of God. He must die for that."

In the morning the priests took Jesus to the Roman ruler, Pilate. Only he could have a person put to death.

"This man Jesus is stirring up a lot of trouble," the priests told Pilate. "You must put him to death!"

Pilate questioned Jesus carefully.

"I can find nothing wrong with him," said Pilate.

Then Pilate asked Jesus, "Are you the king of the Jews?"

"You say so," Jesus answered.

Pilate turned to the crowd who had gathered.

"What shall I do with your king of the Jews? Shall I free him?"

But they all shouted, "To the cross with him! To the cross!"

So Pilate said, "Then I will send him to die on a cross."

The Roman soldiers started to make cruel fun of Jesus. They stuck a crown made out of spiky thorns on his head. They pretended to salute him.

"Long live the king!" they shouted. Then they hit him and spat at him.

Finally the Roman soldiers marched Jesus off to be killed. They led him out through the gates of Jerusalem to a hill called "The Skull".

There they nailed Jesus to a wooden cross. They also put two robbers on crosses. People passing by made fun of Jesus.

"Come down off that cross and save yourself!" they yelled.

But Jesus said, "Father, forgive these people."

At midday the sky suddenly went very dark.
Jesus cried out. Then he died.

A Roman captain standing near the cross said,
"This really was God's Son."

Jesus' family and friends stood and watched sadly.

After Jesus died on the cross, a good man called Joseph went to Pilate.

"Jesus is dead," he said. "May I look after his body?"

The Roman ruler Pilate nodded, "You may!"

So Joseph took Jesus' body from the cross. He wrapped it gently in linen cloth.

Then Joseph laid Jesus' body in a grave carved from rock.

Finally Joseph rolled a huge stone across the doorway, so that Jesus' body would be safe and undisturbed.

Two Roman soldiers stood guarding the door.

John 19

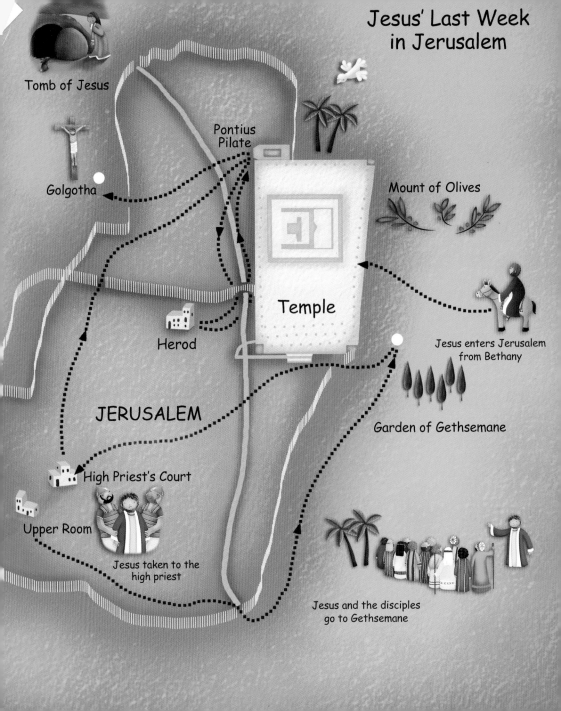

Jesus' Last Week in Jerusalem

Tomb of Jesus

Golgotha

Pontius Pilate

Mount of Olives

Temple

Herod

JERUSALEM

Jesus enters Jerusalem from Bethany

Garden of Gethsemane

High Priest's Court

Upper Room

Jesus taken to the high priest

Jesus and the disciples go to Gethsemane

Jesus is alive!

Early on Sunday morning, while it was still dark, Jesus' friend Mary went to his tomb. She was carrying perfume to put on Jesus' body.

When she arrived, Mary was surprised to see that the big stone in front of the doorway had been rolled back. But she couldn't see Jesus' body.

Mary dashed off back into Jerusalem. She wanted to tell Jesus' friends Peter and John what she had found.

"They've taken away Jesus' body," she cried, "and I can't find it."

Peter and John were very worried. They decided to go to see for themselves and rushed off to the tomb.

John arrived first, as he could run faster than Peter. As soon as he arrived at the door of the tomb, John bent down and peered in.

Out of breath, Peter caught up with John and dashed straight into the tomb. There was no body! The sheets that Jesus had been wrapped in were folded up.

Then John entered the tomb too.
Immediately Peter and John believed that Jesus had risen
from the dead.

Peter and John went back into Jerusalem. But Mary stayed at the tomb, crying. She peered into the tomb again. Through her tears, she saw two angels.

"Why are you crying?" they asked her.

"They've taken Jesus' body away," Mary answered. "And I don't know where it is."

Then Mary turned round and saw Jesus standing there – but she didn't realize it was Jesus.

"Why are you crying?" he asked Mary. "Who are you looking for?"

Mary thought it was the gardener, so she said, "If you've taken away Jesus' body, please tell me where I can find it."

Then Jesus said, "Mary!"
At once Mary knew he was Jesus.
She just said, "Teacher!"
Mary rushed off again to find the disciples, "I've seen Jesus,"
she said. "He's alive!"

John 20

Jesus meets friends at Emmaus

Two of Jesus' followers were walking to Emmaus, a village outside Jerusalem. They felt sad because they still thought Jesus was dead.

As they walked, the two talked about everything that had happened in Jerusalem in the last few days.

Suddenly a stranger started walking along with them. It was Jesus – but the men didn't recognize him.

"What are you talking about?" Jesus asked.

"The things they did to Jesus of Nazareth," they said. "They put him to death. Then some women said they couldn't find his body when they visited his tomb. One said he's alive."

"Why don't you believe these women?" Jesus asked.

When they arrived at their village, the men said to the stranger, "Stay with us; it will soon be dark." So Jesus sat down to supper with them. He took the bread and broke it and gave each of the men a piece.

Suddenly they saw that the stranger was Jesus! At that very moment, he disappeared.

"That was *Jesus*!" said one of the men. "Didn't you feel excited when he was explaining things to us as we were walking along?"

They jumped up and rushed back to Jerusalem, where they found Jesus' disciples.

"It's all true!" they told them. "Jesus really is alive. We've seen him with our own eyes!"

Luke 24

Jesus returns to his Father

Forty days after Jesus rose from the dead, Jesus' special friends, the disciples, were all together in a house in Jerusalem.

Suddenly Jesus appeared in the middle of the room. At first they were frightened.

But Jesus said, "Don't be afraid! God brought me back to life. I want you to go to every country in the world and tell people that God loves them. And tell them about me. You shall be my messengers."

After this Jesus walked with his disciples to the Mount of Olives, just outside Jerusalem. They stood with him on top of the hill.

Jesus said to them, "Now I'm going to be with God. But I am still with you. I always will be."

Then, as Jesus was still talking to them, a cloud came. It took him away. When the cloud disappeared, the disciples couldn't see him any longer. They all stood staring up into the sky.

Suddenly two angels appeared.

"Why are you standing here staring at the sky?" asked the angels. "Jesus is now with God. He will return. Just do what Jesus told you to do."

So the disciples walked back into Jerusalem very happy.

They went to the temple and thanked God for everything that had happened.

Acts 1

The Holy Spirit comes

Jerusalem was full of visitors. Jewish people had come from all over the world to celebrate the festival of Pentecost.

Jesus' followers gathered in a house to pray together.

All of a sudden they heard a roaring noise, like a great, rushing wind. Then they saw tongues of fire moving around the room. The flames settled on each of them. God's Spirit was coming upon them! Jesus' disciples started to speak in different languages.

People outside heard the noise and gathered around the house. Peter went out and preached to them. "You know that Jesus died and was put in a tomb. But he lives! We've seen him with our own eyes. Now he is with God. And he has sent us his Holy Spirit."

Then Peter said: "Believe in Jesus! And be baptized!"
Many of those listening asked to be baptized.
They discovered more about Jesus from the disciples, and became like a big family.

After the Holy Spirit came, Jesus' followers started to do miracles. They told people about God's love and how Jesus had risen from the dead.

One afternoon, Peter and John went to the temple. A disabled man sat begging for money.

Peter looked at him and said, "I don't have any money, but I've something else I can give you: By the power of Jesus stand up and walk!" Up jumped the man. His feet and ankles were now strong.

One day King Herod threw Peter into jail. He wanted to stop Peter telling people about Jesus.

The king ordered sixteen soldiers to guard Peter, who was bound with heavy chains.

That night an angel came to Peter's prison cell. "Quick! Get up!" said the angel. "Put on your coat and follow me." Peter's chains fell off, and the angel led him past the guards. Peter thought he must be dreaming! When they came to the gate of the prison, it swung open and Peter was free.

The angel left him, and Peter hurried to the house of Mary, the mother of John Mark, one of Jesus' followers. Many believers were praying for him inside.

Peter knocked and a girl called Rhoda came to answer. When she heard Peter's voice, she was too excited to open the door – she ran back into the house, shouting, "Peter's here!"

They said, "You're crazy, Rhoda!"

But she insisted it was Peter – who kept on knocking.

When finally they opened the door and saw it *was* him, everyone was amazed.

Acts 2–4, 12

Philip and the Ethiopian

Philip was another of Jesus' followers. He was busy teaching people about Jesus when an angel spoke to him.

"Go along the road to the sea," the angel said.

Philip was on his way when along came an important official from Ethiopia in his chariot. He was reading from the Scriptures.

Philip ran alongside the chariot.

"Do you understand what you're reading?" he asked.

"No, not really," said the Ethiopian. He stopped the chariot and invited Philip to ride with him and explain what the Scriptures meant.

Philip explained the verses the man was reading. They were all about Jesus.

Then the man asked, "Can I get baptized?"

Philip said, "If you believe in Jesus, of course you can."

So they stopped the chariot, and Philip baptized him.
After this, God took Philip to another place.

Acts 8

Paul makes a U-turn

Saul was a devoted Jew from a family of devoted Jews. He went to a Jewish school and had a famous Jewish teacher.

When Saul heard that some Jews were saying Jesus had risen from the dead, it all seemed wrong to him. So Saul decided to help get rid of them.

The chief priests in Jerusalem sent Saul to Damascus to hunt down people who believed in Jesus. He took some armed men with him.

But on the road, something happened. All of a sudden, Saul saw a light that burned so bright that his eyes were blinded. And he heard a voice say, "Saul, why are you hurting me?"

"Who are you?" asked Saul.

"I am Jesus! Now get up and go on to Damascus."

When Saul stood up, he could not see. His men had to lead him into the city.

When he reached Damascus, a follower of Jesus called Ananias found Saul and helped him see again. Ananias explained that Jesus *had* risen from the dead.

Now Saul knew he shouldn't be catching Jesus' followers. Instead, he wanted to tell others that Jesus is alive. Saul changed his name to Paul and started to tell people about Jesus.

It wasn't long before Paul set off on a new adventure. Jesus' followers asked him to travel around telling people about Jesus. So Paul set out with a friend called Barnabas.

First they sailed to the island of Cyprus in the Mediterranean Sea. They visited towns, telling people that Jesus is alive. Many believed and decided to follow Jesus.

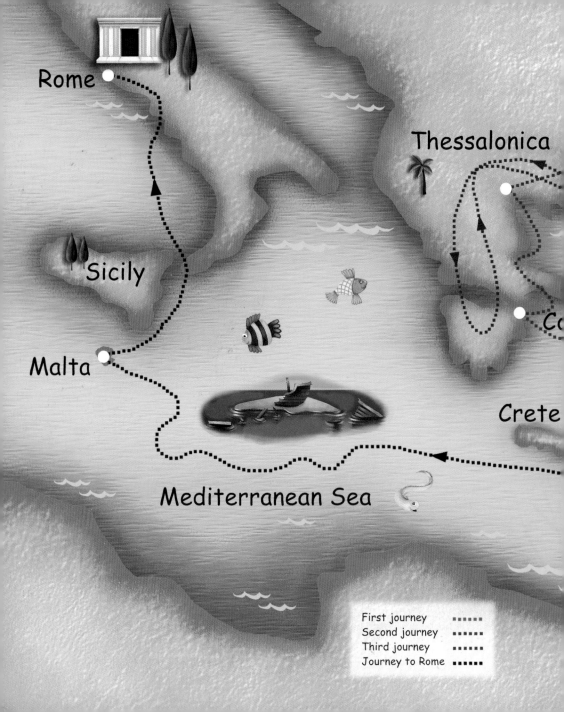

Rome

Thessalonica

Sicily

Co

Malta

Crete

Mediterranean Sea

First journey   ......
Second journey   ......
Third journey   ......
Journey to Rome ■■■■■

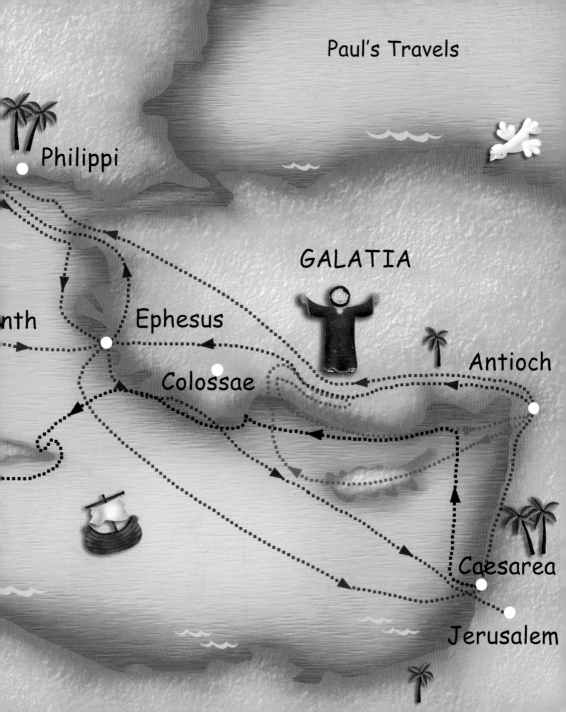

Next Paul and Barnabas went to Asia Minor (the country we now call Turkey). At a town called Iconium so many people believed in Jesus that some of the Jews grew angry – so Paul and Barnabas had to move on to the next town.

Sometimes Paul and Barnabas healed people. At a place called Lystra people were so impressed that they thought Paul and Barnabas were the Greek gods Mercury and Jupiter and tried to worship them. Paul had to explain that it was God who had done the healing.

Soon Paul set off on his travels again. This time, he took another friend – a man called Silas. They visited several more places in Asia Minor.

One night, while he was asleep, Paul saw a man begging him to go to Europe, to take the good news about Jesus.

So Paul found a boat to take them to Macedonia. It was the first time he'd visited Europe.

Paul and Silas went to a town called Philippi, where they found a place to pray beside the river. There they met a woman named Lydia, whose job was to sell expensive purple cloth. She loved God, but didn't know about Jesus.

Paul told her about Jesus, and Lydia came to believe that Jesus is alive. She invited Paul and his friends to stay at her house. Before long a number of people in Philippi became believers.

But some people became angry. They dragged Silas and Paul to court, saying, "These men are disturbing our city!"

Paul and Silas were whipped and thrown into jail. But they knew they were pleasing God, so they spent the night praying and singing hymns!

Suddenly, around midnight, the walls of the jail shook. It was an earthquake! The doors fell open and their chains fell off! The jailer dashed in, thinking everyone had escaped.

"Don't worry!" said Paul. "We're all still here!"

"What must I do to be saved?" the jailer asked.

Paul explained – and he too believed in Jesus.

Paul journeyed on to Athens, in Greece. There he saw an altar with writing on it saying, "TO A GOD WHO IS NOT KNOWN."

So Paul preached to them about the God who created the world.

Paul told the Athenians that God doesn't live in temples built by humans, but lives in people's hearts.

Some laughed at him, but some of the people of Athens believed in Jesus.

Acts 9, 14, 16, 17

A summons from Caesar

After lengthy travels, Paul returned to Jerusalem. He wanted to tell the believers there about his adventures. But some of his enemies saw Paul there and started a riot.

Just in time, some Roman soldiers appeared and rescued Paul. They allowed him to speak to the people. Paul explained how he had met the risen Jesus on the road to Damascus.

But this just stirred the crowd up again, and soon they were shouting "Get rid of Paul! Kill him!"

So the Roman soldiers took Paul into their castle to protect him.

Next day 40 men said they wouldn't eat or drink until they had killed Paul! So the Roman general ordered 200 foot soldiers and 70 horsemen to take Paul safely to the port of Caesarea.

The governor at Caesarea kept Paul in prison. He wanted to find out why all the trouble had arisen. Paul's enemies soon came from Jerusalem asking that he be taken back there for trial.

But Paul said, "I'm a Roman citizen. I demand to be tried in Rome before the emperor himself."

So he was put back in jail until a letter arrived from Rome. The letter ordered him to go to Rome to be tried before the emperor.

Paul was put on a boat going to the port of Myra, in Asia Minor. There he boarded a ship going to Italy.

But winter was approaching, when it was dangerous to sail. Paul's ship could only sail slowly because of the strong winds blowing against it.

Finally, they came to a port. Paul told the captain he thought it would be safer to stay there for a while. But the captain sailed on.

Soon they were caught in a massive storm. For days they didn't see the sun. The sailors couldn't steer the ship. Paul knew they might sink. He told the sailors to eat so they would be strong in the difficult days ahead.

Before long, the ship hit a sandbank and began to break up.
Everyone had to jump into the sea and swim for the beach.
But they all reached shore safely.

The passengers and sailors were shipwrecked on the island of Malta, near Italy. With God's help, no one was drowned.

The islanders were kind to them and built a fire. Paul helped to gather wood. Suddenly a poisonous snake bit him on the hand. Paul shook the snake off into the fire. He wasn't even hurt! God had saved him once again.

Three months later they continued the voyage to Rome in another ship.

At last they arrived in the great city of Rome.

In Rome, Paul was kept under guard until his trial.
He wrote letters to his friends in Asia Minor and Greece.

While he was in Rome a runaway slave called Onesimus visited Paul. He came to believe in Jesus.

A runaway slave could be punished; and, of course, Paul didn't want that to happen to Onesimus. So Paul told him to return to his master, Philemon, who also believed in Jesus, and gave him a letter to take with him.

Paul spent years in prison. He was probably executed by Emperor Nero in Rome.

But the good news he preached about Jesus went on spreading throughout the world.

Acts 21–28, Philemon 1